The Wanda Way

The managerial philosophy and values of one of China's largest companies

WANG JIANLIN

Published by
LID Publishing Limited
One Adam Street, London WC2N 6LE

31 West 34th Street, Suite 7004,
New York, NY 10001, U.S.

info@lidpublishing.com
www.lidpublishing.com

A member of:

www.businesspublishersroundtable.com

The Wanda Way is translated from the original Chinese edition 万达哲学

Printed in Great Britain by TJ International
ISBN: 978-1-910649-42-8
ISBN: 978-1-910649-64-0 (Airport Edition)

Page design: Caroline Li

The Wanda Way

The managerial philosophy and values of one of China's largest companies

WANG JIANLIN

LONDON MONTERREY
MADRID SHANGHAI
MEXICO CITY BOGOTA
NEW YORK BUENOS AIRES
BARCELONA SAN FRANCISCO

Preface 1

Most business schools have, among their objectives, the promotion of entrepreneurship. Entrepreneurs are the best engines of a successful society. Through the formation of new companies they create lots of jobs, they increase the quality of life for many people, they pay taxes, and through all of this they contribute to a much better and fairer society.

We need to study entrepreneurs to learn how to do this well. Business schools write case studies and books on entrepreneurs and invite them to speak in an attempt to understand what makes an entrepreneur and to formalize and spread this knowledge to students.

There is no doubt that Mr. Wang Jianlin is an entrepreneur. He started work as a Public Office Administrator, then he moved to management, and ended up launching a start-up with a relatively small amount of money. This is the entrepreneurial career of somebody who learns every day, has honest ambition to progress, and works hard.

Entrepreneurs have the capability to identify an opportunity and transform this opportunity into business, but this requires commitment, capacity to take risks, and a professional way of moving from opportunity to start-up and then to a fast-growing company. When you look at entrepreneurs like Wang Jianlin you see that many of the opportunities he transformed into business were there and many other people passed by without really working on them. An entrepreneur has a special ability to detect potential, but also the capacity to follow up closely, fix mistakes quickly, and stick to a good business plan model.

The book on Wang Jianlin is an excellent contribution. Society needs good entrepreneurs all over the world. We must be grateful to Wang Jianlin for all that he has contributed to the world, creating jobs and enthusiasm and setting a good example. Now, through this book, we have better access to knowledge about how to become an entrepreneur. This is a very solid reason to thank Wang Jianlin.

Dr Pedro Nueno
President, Chengwei Ventures Chair Professor of Entrepreneurship, CEIBS, China

Preface 2

It is my honor to be invited to write the preface to this book that documents the unique success of Wang Jianlin, chairman of Wanda and one of the great entrepreneurs of the early twenty-first century.

That Wang is currently the wealthiest man in Asia is intriguing. What business skills enabled him to achieve this level of success in just 27 years? More important is the man himself. From where does Wang draw his inspiration? How does he balance his work and his life? What can he teach us, not just about how to make money, but how to live a good life as a Chinese entrepreneur?

In *The Wanda Way*, Wang reveals in his own words, the subtleties of his leadership style. He openly shares how he achieves balance between the old and the new models of management, between envisioning the future and managing the day-to-day, between competitive pressures, consumer trends and political realities.

In practical terms, *The Wanda Way* offers the Western reader insights on several important topics: how to sustain an entrepreneurial spirit in an increasingly large organization; how to remain alert to competition, despite the risk of complacency flowing from success;

how to repeatedly reinvent a company's strategy in the face of changing market forces, not once but four times; how to inculcate a culture of continuous improvement and innovation; how to embrace the opportunities of e-commerce and the digital world, while getting the timing right; and how to build the brand promise of Wanda at home and abroad.

As Wang says, the greatest rewards come from pursuing spiritual goals. The highest level of enterprise management is creating and sustaining an outstanding corporate culture. Wanda's core values have enabled the company to survive and prosper through four strategic transformations. More will no doubt follow, as Wanda becomes an ever-greater presence on the international stage.

John A.Quelch
Charles Edward Wilson Professor of Business Administration,
Harvard Business School

Contents

Preface 1 by Pedro Nueno 4
Preface 2 by John A. Quelch 6
Foreword: Wang Jianlin's Biography 14

CHAPTER 1 25
Perseverance

Perseverance Breeds Success
Every person has a shot at succeeding, but in order to achieve it you need to seek out undiscovered opportunities and be innovative. Apart from that, the most important qualities are to never give up, not to be afraid of failure, to keep on learning and to keep on fighting in spite of all setbacks.
29 April, 2013 – Guest appearance on China Central Television's "Voice"

CHAPTER 2 43
Determination

Where There's a Will, There's a Way
In spite of how amazing a company appears to be, distinction does not occur after you have grown big, but at the time you have just started. The ambition to create something amazing is the kind of feeling an entrepreneur has from the very beginning, and success is not attainable without it. These genes are implanted into a company's DNA right from the outset.
22 June, 2013 – A Speech at Huashang College

Creating Smart Shopping Malls

A little more than one third of China's consumer market goes in a shopping bag. But nearly two thirds can neither be carried in a bag, nor be sold online. This is the larger market: the consumption of experiences – watching movies, dining out, entertainment and more. We have spoken of the need to create an e-commerce platform catered to such a market.

29 August, 2014 – Speech from the Strategic Cooperation Agreement Signing Ceremony for Wanda E-Commerce

Promoting Philanthropy in our Corporate Culture

Wanda ensures that funds are allocated each year for charitable donations. For the past three years we've set aside 400 million yuan a year towards public welfare initiatives. We encourage everyone in our company to volunteer at least once a year, ensuring the spirit of philanthropy and giving back to society remains alive throughout the company.

16 August, 2014 – Statement at the First China Charity Forum

Wang Jianlin's Biography

Building up a company from scratch to become China's and Asia's richest man took Wanda Group chairman Wang Jianlin just 27 years. As a first generation entrepreneur of China's reform and opening-up, Wang Jianlin seized the great opportunities created by the country's economic takeoff. With his keen and rich vision, adeptness in innovation and strong will power, he persevered with his principles and exhibited the flexibility to go through many changes. Now, he's a giant – a modern day J.P. Morgan or Rockefeller commanding a pivotal role and respect in the business world.

I. Early Career and Pioneering Days

Wang Jianlin, the eldest son in his family, was born in Sichuan province on 24 October 1954. His father was a member of the Red Army and took part in the Long March. When he was 15, Wang Jianlin entered the military and became a soldier in a northern China border garrison. Wang Jianlin, of a competitive nature, always remembered how his mother impressed upon him the need to be a good soldier. He persevered with the 1,000-kilometer march and upon arriving at the Snowy Forest with the troops, he became one of only a small number of soldiers to complete this arduous task. Before he was 30, Wang Jianlin became a regiment officer. He was the youngest officer among hundreds of thousands of troops. The 17-year military career had a profound impact on Wang Jianlin's life. After his military career, Wanda was often likened to the military because of its invincibility in battle and execution in business.

In 1986, shortly after China's reform and opening-up began, Wang Jianlin realized that China's future would shift, with economic construction moving to the fore, so he decided to give up the dream of becoming a general and change jobs. He went to the Xigang district of Dalian and became an official. Because of his outstanding performance he was promoted quickly and became the office director. A promising future beckoned. In the 1980s, reform-minded government officials formed businesses in waves. These people became China's first generation of entrepreneurs. Wang Jianlin was deeply affected by this and was no longer satisfied working in a quiet office. He was eager for more challenges and for a better life. In 1988, an opportunity that changed Wang Jianlin's life presented itself. A newly established Xigang district real estate company was on the verge of bankruptcy due to poor management. In order to save the company, the district government looked to the community to recruit someone. Wang Jianlin volunteered; he resigned from his government position and became the general manager of the company. This company was the predecessor of today's Wanda Group.

To keep the company alive, Wang Jianlin looked everywhere he could for development projects, but at that time policy restrictions made it very difficult to find a good project. In 1989 Wang Jianlin decided to accept the government-recommended "Dalian Beijing Street Urban Renewal Project." Because this project was not expected to be profitable, other powerful enterprises refused to take it, but Wang Jianlin decided to take the gamble. He shattered the existing housing construction conventions and designed bigger and better units, using aluminum windows instead of the traditional wooden ones and installing security doors on each household. These innovations enabled the sale of more than 800 units within two months. The prices created a record in Dalian, and Wang Jianlin dug into the first pot of gold. This single transaction gave Wang Jianlin a taste of the sweetness of innovation, and he saw the opportunities in urban renewal. Since then, he has been unstoppable.

Deeply influenced by Confucian ideology, Wang Jianlin attaches great importance to integrity. He often quotes the Confucian saying, "If people have no faith in a person, there is no standing for that person." He believes that in the business world, integrity is "eating a small loss for a big deal." Early in his real estate career the Chinese real estate market was completely chaotic, fraud was commonplace, and housing quality was inferior. Wang Jianlin was resolute in not following the bad examples of others. In his company he presented the saying, "conduct oneself honestly and handle matters astutely." He required that all residences constructed by Wanda met the country's first-rate engineering standards and made his famous three commitments: Wanda houses bought by consumers are refundable and exchangeable, and should a leakage or square footage shortage occur, generous compensation would be granted. Wang Jianlin's efforts paid off, and Wanda earned the reputation as a supplier of good houses. Wanda flourished in Dalian and occupied almost one quarter of the local real estate market.

II. Innovation and Transformation

Among various factors that led to Wang's success, innovation and transformation were the most important ones.

The first transformation made Wanda, originally a local company, into a nationwide enterprise. Obtaining success in one city was not enough to satisfy Wang Jianlin. He wanted Wanda to become a famous national enterprise. In 1992 Deng Xiaoping delivered his famous speech while touring southern China, ushering in a new round of entrepreneurialism. Wanda then expanded out of Dalian and went to Guangzhou, the most economically developed city in China, for development projects. This made Wanda China's first real estate company to develop cross-regionally. Although the project was not very profitable, it gave Wang Jianlina lot of confidence. Years later, Wanda rapidly expanded throughout the entire country.

At this time Wang Jianlin established China's first professional football club; the team is a testament to Wang Jianlin's great ambitions. In five years the team won the League Championship four times with a record of 55 consecutive unbeaten games, a record no team has been able to break. The success has made Wang Jianlin and Wanda well known nationwide and paved the way for advancement into the sports industry.

The second transformation was that from residential properties to commercial properties. Despite the company's success, Wang Jianlin still had a very strong sense of crisis. This feeling was caused by the Chinese real estate market's extreme fluctuations and the commitment he felt to his employees. He wanted to give the entrepreneurial comrades who were following him a sense of security and access to medical services. Wang Jianlin looked for an industry with a stable long-term cash flow.

In May 2000, Wanda held the "Zunyi Conference," which would become decisive in shaping the development of the company. Against all objections, Wang Jianlin announced that Wanda would make the transition from residential to commercial real estate. However, a lack of experience made it difficult for Wanda. Media criticism, litigation from investors, and internal skepticism ensued. Under tremendous pressure, Wang Jianlin went through 222 lawsuits, of which one project had to be demolished and reconstructed, as it could not be saved due to design reasons. With a loss of 1.5 billion yuan, this affair went down in history as a representative of Chinese corporate integrity. Wang Jianlin gritted his teeth and persevered for five years, until developing a comprehensive city business model for the Chinese economy. In 2006, within a period of 12 months, Wanda successfully opened Ningbo's Yinzhou, Shanghai's Wujiaochang, Beijing's CBD and three other Wanda Plazas, obtaining the leading position in China's real estate field. In 2008, Wang Jianlin moved his corporate headquarters from Dalian to the nation's capital of Beijing, where it now occupies a prominent position in Beijing's Central Business District. In the following few years, Wanda opened more than 20 large Wanda Plazas per year and each year saw an annual increase of several million square meters of commercial area. This pace of growth came to be known as "Wanda speed." In 2015 Wanda officially became the world's largest scale real estate company. In retrospect, Wang Jianlin summarized the keys to this as innovation and perseverance.

Real estate development brought about more business opportunities for Wang Jianlin. He started the third transformation by heavily investing in the cultural tourism industry. Because Wanda Plazas needed cinemas, Wanda entered the cinematic world, and luckily enough benefited from the explosion of the Chinese film market. Within five years it became China's biggest cinematic chain. The unexpected success allowed Wang Jianlin to see the potential of China's cultural industry. In his words, it is an industry "with no ceilings."

In 2008, Wanda developed the first integrated culture-based business and integrated tourism project – the Wuhan Central Cultural Zone, the total investment for which reached 50 billion yuan. Two projects that make Wang Jianlin very proud happen to be the world's leading cultural projects – the Han Show and Cinema Park. Wang Jianlin, an adept innovator, has integrated culture, business and tourism to launch a massive Wanda Cultural Tourism City. This ambitious project utilizes an indoor cultural entertainment project that can be played in throughout the year as well as a large-scale outdoor theme park, a group of resorts and much more. The investments for each project surpass 20 billion yuan, and ten have already been started. Wang Jianlin plans to spread them globally, keep up with Disney and allow a Chinese cultural brand to triumph internationally.

Early in 2012, a high-spirited Wang Jianlin turned his gaze towards the whole world. That same year he took over AMC and became the world's largest cinema-chain operator. Later he took over Australia's HOYTS Cinema to further expand his cinema network. Wanda took over the United Kingdom's famous Sunseeker Yachts business and is starting construction on Wanda Hotels in the central districts of London, Madrid, Los Angeles, Chicago, Sydney and the Gold Coast.

In the sports field, Wang Jianlin has taken over Switzerland's Infront Sports and Media Group, purchased 20% of the Atletico Madrid football club and acquired America's World Triathlon Corporation. In just one year it became the world's largest whole-industry chain-sports management company. Large-scale mergers and acquisitions have allowed Wang Jianlin to become a world famous entrepreneur. More and more American, European, and Asian politicians and entrepreneurs are going to his office in Beijing recommending projects and lobbying for investments.

III. Social Responsibility through Charity

In China, Wang Jianlin is known widely as a philanthropist. He made "creating wealth together, sharing with society" a corporate mission and is the first in China to have proposed pursuing a social enterprise. He believes development of enterprise is not only for one's self, but more for its social contribution. He strives for the creation of wealth to ultimately return it to society. Because he adheres to this philosophy, Wang Jianlin has contributed more than four billion yuan to poverty alleviation, education, disaster relief and other areas. He is one of the largest contributing entrepreneurs in China, and is honored because of this. Wang Jianlin is Vice-Chairman of Harvard University's Global Advisory Board and is the Honorary President of the China Charity Federation. He and his company have already won the country's highest philanthropic honour, the China Charity Award, seven times. The award is for outstanding contributions in the field of poverty alleviation. The China State Council named him the "National Advanced Individual for Poverty Alleviation." Wang Jianlin's contributions to society are recognized at the political level. He served as a representative on the 17th Communist Party of China (CPC) National Congress, is a member of the standing committee of the Chinese People's Political Consultative Conference (CPPCC) National Committee, and is the Vice-Chairman of the All China Federation of Industry and Commerce.

In the early days, Wang Jianlin displayed a strong concern for social welfare, and in 1990, under less than affluent circumstances, Wang Jianlin for the first time donated one million yuan to build a kindergarten. In Dalian, he donated the city Plaza, stadiums, schools and more. He was devoted to helping a poverty-stricken village in Dalian, and provided assistance until the village overcame poverty completely.

When society encounters a difficult situation, Wang Jianlin is always the first to contribute and drive other entrepreneurs to participate in relief. He was the first to donate in the Wenchuan earthquake in Sichuan province in 2008, and his contribution amounted to 350 million yuan; immediately after the 2010 Qinghai earthquake in Yushu County, he donated 100 million yuan.

Education is the focus of Wang Jianlin's charity events. It has become customary at Wanda to contribute to the construction of a local school at the beginning of each property development. Now hundreds of Hope primary and secondary schools have been built across the country. In 1994, Wanda invested 500 million yuan towards the building of Dalian University, which covers an area of 1.06 million square meters and constitutes an area of 300,000 square meters of building. In 2010, Wanda contributed 200 million yuan to the construction of a senior high school in Chengdu; in 2014 Wanda contributed 100 million yuan to the construction of Sichuan Guang yuan Wanda Middle School.

To help revitalize weak Chinese football, Wang Jianlin invested 600 million yuan. His investment went to hiring a high-level international coach for the national football team, providing funds for the women's league, organizing the youth football league and so on. Among these, the most important is the annual selection of 30 outstanding Chinese youth football players to study abroad in Spain's three best youth training clubs, allowing Chinese football to develop talent.

Wang Jianlin's long-term desire is the eradication of poverty, and many of his contributions are to help poor farmers. In 2015, Wang Jianlin implemented a massive poverty alleviation project. He pledged to help Danzhai county in Guizhou province to wholly overcome poverty. The county has more than 50,000 farmers living below the poverty line. Wang Jianlin created a five-year plan to invest 1 billion yuan, through which a local tea-processing industry and an occupational college will be constructed, among other measures. This plan will help these people to completely overcome poverty within five years.

In order to help Chinese university students in entrepreneurship and train the next generation of Chinese entrepreneurs, Wang Jianlin has implemented a decade-long Collegiate Business Plan, which provides financial aid to 100 university students each year. The shops with the best locations in Wanda Plazas are these students' entrepreneurial bases, and arrangements are made for professionals to give business counseling.

Under Wang Jianlin's leadership, charity has become part of Wanda's corporate culture. Wanda has a special system, in which all Wanda companies have established volunteer stations, and all Wanda employees have become volunteers and must volunteer at least once a year. Wang Jianlin hopes that through this method, each employee will have the right attitude.

IV. Following the Dream and Daring to Persevere

Wang Jianlin is now China's most successful entrepreneur. The success he has achieved has already far surpassed what he originally imagined. Wanda is the world's largest real estate company, the world's largest five-star hotel owner, and has the world's largest chain cinema company. Wanda Sports is the world's largest sports industry company. He's still not content. His dream now is to create a great enterprise that can continue in greatness after he has left the company, thus changing the world's perception of Chinese companies – and all for the honor of China.

In 2015, Wang Jianlin began Wanda's fourth transformation. As far as Wanda is concerned, this will be comprehensive and profound. His goal is to establish a business empire built on four services – retail, culture, finance and e-commerce – which will all be global leaders. At the same time, he aims to complete a comprehensive restructuring of his business from real estate to a service-oriented business. He wants to move beyond being a real estate tycoon and become a global business leader. His target objectives are all global industry giants, but the goal is to subvert the old pattern. He wants to open 1,000 Wanda Plazas in China, allowing Wanda to enter each Chinese city with a population of 300,000 or more to cover nearly 1 billion people. This will be the world's largest business platform. In the film and television industry, his objective is to create a global film supply chain and break Hollywood's monopoly in the film industry, allowing the global spread of Chinese culture. In sports, he will bulk purchase core resources to change the world's professional sports industry and become an important force in the rules of the game. In tourism, Wang Jianlin not only wants to become the world's largest, but also wants to spread Wanda's cultural tourism cities globally and keep up with Disney. He wants Wanda to become a world-renowned hotel brand. In the area of e-commerce, he is creating the largest global integrated online to offline e-commerce platform. By 2020, Wanda's enterprise market value and assets are required to reach US$200 billion with revenue of US$100 billion and a net profit of US$10 billion. The contribution of overseas revenue will be 30%, allowing Wanda to become a first-rate world multinational corporation. To achieve this, 61-year-old Wang Jianlin knows no rest. Just as in the Dalian venture, provided he is not travelling for business, each day he is on time in the office at 7 a.m. to begin a busy day's work. However, due to the worldwide nature of business, he must now spend more time on flights and cope with jet lag. In order to stay in good shape, he is cultivating jogging as a new hobby and has actually lost weight.

Wang Jianlin once summarized the keys to his success as innovation and perseverance: "I believe that with good innovative ideas, a good innovative approach, and a lot of perseverance, success is a certainty." Now he talks more about dreams; he says in life you must give yourself an ambitious goal and work hard. The stage will be as large as the amount of heart you have. Nobody knows where his limit lies, but everyone believes he will have a great influence on his times.

Chapter One

Perseverance

Perseverance Breeds Success

29 April, 2013 – China Central Television *Voice*, featuring Wang Jianlin

During his guest appearance on *Voice*, a well-known weekly program produced by China Central Television, Wang Jianlin gave a keynote speech entitled "Perseverance is the Key to Success" and answered questions from an audience of university students.

In his speech, he shared stories of his upbringing illustrating this maxim with insightful personal anecdotes and the history of Wanda Group.

Here is what he had to say:

"I was asked to set the topic for this talk today and have settled on 'success requires perseverance.' I was only 15 or 16 when, in 1970, I did my military service. 1970 was the year when Chairman Mao issued the '24 November' instruction, intoning that 'camp and field training is good.' Once the instruction had been relayed that day, we would set out in the evening, each of us shouldering a bag of grain and a rucksack. On top of that, we had another 10 kilograms or so to carry. We began our training across more than 1,000 kilometers. The northeast really was forests of trees and knee-deep stretches of snow. We slept in the open. We were deprived of everything. In the snow, we had to dig our own hole to spend the night. We walked a daily average of 30 kilometers.

Some days 35 or 40 kilometers. If you could not cope, you could go sit in the car at the back, which was emblazoned 'sag wagon.' However, if you did that, you could forget about being chosen to move up that year or earning your Exemplary Fighter award. This kind of hardship is difficult for today's youth to imagine.

During regular training, perhaps the regular rations were sufficient, but being as cold as it was, and exerting yourself that much, you still felt hungry even if you ate more. At that time, my squad leader said to me: 'Wang, I want to tell you something, about how to eat your fill, but first you need to promise you will keep it secret.' I told him I would never tell anyone. In those days, the soldiers used a bowl to eat, a big, tall, crude bowl. He said: 'When you go up there to fill your bowl, first fill it up only half. No matter how slowly you eat, you will still finish your rice before the others and you can have seconds. You can then fill your bowl to the brim, and you won't feel hungry. By all means, never foolishly fill up your bowl at the first serving – as many are tempted to do – because when they go back for seconds, there is no rice left.' I never forgot his tip, and even though I was very young, that year on the road as a soldier, I was basically never hungry.

How tough was our camp and field training? I saw with my own eyes how a cadre was sitting there crying, saying he had had it. 'I am not walking another step. I don't want my Party membership. I don't care about being a cadre!' Many of us could not keep up. Of a team of over 1,000 marching, not more than 400 reached the end. As a young teenager, I held on until the end. What kept me going was a conviction. When I started out, my mother told me, 'You must become an Exemplary Fighter. Your father too served in the army, and you should strive to surpass him.' This kind of conviction and persistence allowed me to join the army the first year and become an Exemplary Fighter.

Therefore, whatever you undertake in life won't be successful unless you have a teeth-gritting spirit and a desire to fight until the end. This is a theme I have been talking about for over ten years: perseverance lies at the core of the entrepreneurial spirit. First, no innovation, no dream can be achieved without perseverance. I started my company in 1988. In those days, I already had a really good life. In my early twenties,

I had become a regiment-level officer. That was a really nice time in my official career. Those were the days – in the late 80s and early 90s – when there was a big wave of start-ups in China, and when many people tried their hands at a new trade. I was affected by the trend and decided that I too wanted to start up a company and realize my dream.

The industry I chose in those days is one probably loathed by many today – real estate. When I had chosen my industry, what I needed next was a registered capital. We reached an agreement with a state-owned enterprise in Dalian to give us a loan. But with only money, we might not yet have been able to find a place because for that you needed to have a quota issued by the State Planning Commission. We did not have a quota. What could we do?

I found another state-owned company, one of the three largest real estate companies in Dalian. I knew that one of my old comrades was the president there. So I talked to him. Would he be prepared to lend me his quota? Of course, I understood full well that borrowing his quota would cost money. There I was, with half a million in cash and with a quota I started my real estate business from a building. The start was far from glorious. On the contrary, it was really tough. I still remember the kind of grinding and discrimination I had to put up with as a private entrepreneur. For a loan of 20 million yuan – which by the way had already been promised to us by that bank – I must have run back and forth over 50 times. I confronted the bank manager in person, until he did want to see me. I knew what time he started work and would go to intercept him every day. As I was always standing near the entrance, he possibly got in through another entrance. Sometimes I waited for him at lunchtime. I thought he might go back to work after his noon nap, so I would wait for him at his office's entrance. I clearly knew he was inside yet his secretary said that he was out or asked me to wait. It came to the point that I knew his home address and caught him on his way home in the evening. In the morning, he'd wake up and look out of the window. When he saw me waiting downstairs, he would rather stay at home to avoid having to face me. This went on for a while. I ran back and forth dozens of times. But in the end, he did not grant me that loan.

So I set myself a target: I want my company to be big, to be the best in the world!

Secondly, success is a process of ongoing improvement, and the key to it is nothing but perseverance. Without appropriate planning, we encountered many detours from 2000 – when we had just expanded into the commercial property market – to 2004. During this period, we were named as a defendant in 222 lawsuits, which made it virtually impossible for us to focus on and grow our business. Some of my colleagues were under extreme pressure from public opinion. I was asked at that time why we had to enter the commercial property business since we had seen such great success in the residential property sector. In the face of all this, I wavered many times. I then set a goal for my team and myself: we will keep going till the five-year mark, and if we are still struggling at the end of 2005, we will exit the commercial property market. It was our perseverance during those times that enabled us to successfully launch our third-generation Wanda Plaza. Given the opening and success of the Shanghai Wujiaochang Plaza, Ningbo Yinzhou Plaza and Beijing CBD Plaza, we have fully established our confidence in continuing to be an active player in the commercial property sector.

By the end of 2014, we expect to own 20 million square meters of commercial real estate. It is likely that we will overtake the world's No.1 real estate developer, the U.S.-based Simon Company, in terms of commercial space. It has taken us 15 years to get there, as compared to more than 100 years for the Simon Company. We have to realize that without perseverance and ongoing pursuit of our desired goal, there would be no way for us to leave those struggles and failures behind.

Another story that I'd like share with you is about the Shenyang Taiyuan Street Wanda Plaza. At that time, we engaged two commercial property experts in China to help design a pedestrian street to bring in customer flow. However, several hundred clients who purchased our retail spaces brought a class action against us because only 3-5% of them registered satisfactory returns, and most of them recorded extremely low or virtually non-existent returns. Although we won the lawsuit eventually, which meant that we were not obliged to take responsibility for their losses, I insisted on not letting our clients down. We first brought in a group of experts, on whose advice we spent tens of millions to install a canopy to shield against rain and snow to improve the business performance of our clients. Later, they advised us to put in several escalators leading to the basement to increase traffic. Both attempts failed.

Then, we were told that we picked the wrong buyers, so we had them replaced. Almost four years passed and nothing changed. We reached a consensus at last within the Group that this project was doomed to fail if we didn't demolish it with explosives. This meant that, in addition to refunding our clients, we would have to pay out 1 billion yuan in compensation as well as the cost of the demolition itself, coming to at least 1.5 billion yuan in total. We decided eventually to compensate our space buyers at 150% of the purchase price and rebuild the project.

Don't jump to the conclusion that you are successful simply because you have an innovative idea or rack up some early success. For example, running a small noodle restaurant successfully may give you the impulse to open a chain restaurant. However, if you really do start your own chain, you might end up failing because of not being able to adapt to the required changes, as running a chain requires a solid management model and putting together a good team. Most of you are university students and may have just left campus. Many of you dream of having your own business and achieving success. Every single one of you has the chance to succeed, and the first key is to understand how you can differentiate yourself from others and to be innovative. What is even more important is to be persistent and never yield to failures.

I've always said that ambition never dies until there is no way out. Why? Because solutions are always there for the problems we face. Success can be ours only if we are persistent.

This concludes my speech. Thank you very much."

Q&A

Sa Beining (host): Let's applaud him again for such an inspiring speech,Mr. Wang Jianlin. Thank you! During your speech, many students sent their questions and many of them are very interesting indeed. First, let me ask you, we can ask any questions, right?

Wang Jianlin: Yes, any questions.

Sa: Is your promise as good as gold?

Wang Jianlin: As good as silver, at least.

Sa: So a long time ago you promised the old squad leader to keep his secret, but you told us all here today. Why? He asked you not to tell anyone, not even a single person. Today, all Chinese people have heard it.

Wang Jianlin: Things were different back then. We now have enough to eat these years.

Sa: So it did matter back then?

Wang Jianlin: Yes.

Sa: And now it doesn't matter any more?

Wang Jianlin: No, not any more.

Sa: The next question is a tricky one. I heard that you once said that if the boss of a company went mountain climbing all the time, you didn't think that he could manage the company successfully. I know that a real estate entrepreneur by the name of Wang Shi is fond of mountaineering, so did you say that as an allusion to Wang Shi?

Wang Jianlin: I've never said anything like that. If I did, it would be a personal insult.

Sa: ...to Wang Shi for sure.

Wang Jianlin: Wang Shi and I are pretty good friends...You're obviously trying to sow discord between us with this question.

Sa: Not me, not me...

Wang Jianlin: It's such an unkind thing to ask.

Sa: But Wang Shi once said that if the boss of a company criticized others all the time for being obsessed with mountain climbing, he would doubt that he could ever run the business successfully. Well...I made this up. But you really didn't make that remark (about mountain climbing)?

Wang Jianlin: No, I didn't…no way. It's just that someone told me that I worked too hard, and I should relax more…it was possible to enjoy life and manage a successful company at the same time. I said I didn't believe that anyone can run a successful business while relaxing at work. Perhaps (it's because) I always believed in the three key factors for success that someone said before, which are talent, hard work and opportunity. Hence, hard work is part of the formula.

Sa: Next, we have eight young representatives on the stage here, and they'll ask you questions from different professional perspectives. Ma Li, please.

Ma Li: Hi, Mr. Wang Jianlin. It's great to meet you. My name is Ma Li. I'm from the University of Nottingham Ningbo China. You just mentioned the three major campaigns and Yinzhou Wanda Plaza in Ningbo was one of them. I'm very excited because the plaza is very close to our university. During my university days, I went there many times to dine with classmates, take my girlfriend on dates, sing and shop. Seeing you really moved and excited me. Why? The customer is king. I finally met the man who sold me the movie tickets for the first time in my life.

I liked your speech very much because as a business student myself I found the knowledge and case studies you shared with us very interesting. However, one thing I didn't like is that your speech was a bit too serious, and it didn't feel like we were appearing on a TV show. It was more like a global board meeting in Wanda Group. You were the chairman, Sa Beining was the president and the rest of us were all regional managers…and we were talking about if we'd be paid one million yuan for this year.

Sa: I was wondering how much the president would be paid.

Ma Li: More than one million…that's for sure. Now my question is don't you have any tender feelings at all in life?

Wang Jianlin: Perhaps I'm not a take-it-easy kind of person as some other entrepreneurs are…I'm relatively more serious, but it doesn't mean that I can't have a kind heart. I'm very sentimental. Many of my old comrades and friends would tell you the truth that I always keep some cash in my office safe…as I always have visitors telling me that they met me before, but I can't remember who they are. I often ask them what they are visiting me for, and the answers are usually that they've got financial difficulties. I give them some money straight away, and I've never expected repayment.

Ma Li: I also believe what you just said…that you treat friends, comrades and people in need with a kind heart…a soft heart,but you didn't mention if you treat your employees at work with a tender heart. For example, I feel for the eight representatives or your regional managers, your speech is awe-inspiring as well as unnerving, but we couldn't feel the personal touch. This made me I wonder if, given such an attitude, your employees dare to tell you their true feelings?

Wang Jianlin: You're right on this point. I'm very serious at work, and I think there are few people in the company that dare to tell me what they really think. I'm being honest with you about this. Especially junior-level and ordinary employees who rarely get the chance, so only some veterans of the company who have followed me during the past decade or so and seven or eight close friends of mine…they're always straight-forward with me (if they disagree with me).

Ma Li: You just said that whoever met you could go to your office and ask for money. Next time we meet I could say, Mr. Wang, we met on the Voice…give me some money, please.

Wang Jianlin: If you can see me and manage to sell me on your idea, it's okay. If you really want to start your own business, then you need to send your proposition, and we'll ask three evaluators to assess your report. As for the other things you mentioned, I'll do my best to improve.

Ma Li: I've made up my mind on the kind of business I'd like to run in the future. That is, to tackle problems involved with communications between successful entrepreneurs and their subordinates. This will be the focus of my business. Thank you.

Sa: It's a pretty good idea.

Wang Jianlin: A good idea, and it may work out indeed.

Sa: Next, Wang Xichen.

Wang Xichen: Hi, uncle Wang. Ma Li just said that he was frightened of you because you looked very serious, but I felt an intimate connection when I met you today. Why? Because my father is also named Wang Jianlin, so when I saw you today you reminded me of my father.

Sa: This is your father's ID card?

Wang Xichen: Yes.

Sa: But the character jian (健) in the middle is different from that of yours (建). I think the jian as in jian-shuo (健硕 which means strong) suits you better.

Wang Jianlin: My mother named me with *jian* at first. I changed it to *jian* when I joined the army. What a coincidence!

Sa: What does your father do?

Wang Xichen: By coincidence, my father is also in business.

Wang Jianlin: We may meet someday.

Wang Xichen: My father is a very daring and courageous man.

Sa: So you didn't take advantage of that name claiming that…

Wang Xichen: I'm too shy sometimes and have lost some opportunities because of it. For example, during a class leader election, the teacher asked us three times who would volunteer for the post of class monitor. Each time I raised my hand like this, but I was too shy to stretch it out…I thought to myself that I would raise my hand when the teacher asked for the third time, but when it came and I was ready to raise my hand, my desk mate did it ahead of me and he was elected class monitor. The question I want to ask you is if you can teach us how to embolden ourselves within the shortest time possible. Is there some shortcut to doing this?

Wang Jianlin: There are no shortcuts. The only way to achieve this is through practice. The first time I appeared on a TV show, I was too shy to speak logically. The first time I sang in public, I was pushed onto the stage…I didn't realize that I was tone deaf until I started the song. The audience laughed their heads off…If there's a shortcut to success, it's practice. There's no such thing as shortcuts, otherwise my autobiography would be a bestseller. If you're afraid of speaking in public, you won't improve it unless you practice it in front of people. Currently, there is a saying that EQ (Emotion Quotient) is the key to success. Learning to get along with other people helps us most to achieve success.

Sa: We're sometimes afraid of doing something, but once we bite the bullet and do it for the first time, we're surprised about how good it felt. If you raised your hand that day, you'd be the class monitor now.

Wang Jianlin: I've never met anyone with the same name as mine. Tell your father to send me an e-mail. We can arrange a time to meet, seriously.(2)

Wang Zhen: The central theme of your speech today is perseverance, but I think certain types of perseverance are questionable. One of the graduates from my college was an enthusiastic mountaineer and had pursued his mountaineer career ever since graduation. Unfortunately, he died in an accident while climbing a mountain last year at the age of 28. At his funeral, his parents said that we support youngsters today to pursue their dreams, but you should also put yourselves in your parents' shoes. You're not living only for yourselves. So my question is do you think such perseverance is worth it?

Wang Jianlin: Entrepreneurship is a spiritual ideal, and we need to make sensible psychological preparations.

Sa: Perseverance should be based on sensible analysis.

Wang Jianlin: Exactly, exactly.

Sa: There's a man in Chinese history known for his perseverance, the man who stands by a tree stump waiting for a hare. He is persevering but is only remembered as a negative example.

Ma Li: I can't agree with Wang Zhen on this point. I think it's just one of the rare cases, and I feel that there are different types of perseverance. In some cases, perseverance is advisable, and some of our dreams must be changed, where perseverance is not advisable. If J.K. Rowling gave up her dream after numerous rejections by the publishers year after year, Harry Potter would have never been published. If Walt Disney gave up after the idea of a theme park was dismissed by the banks and other people, there wouldn't be any Disneyland in the world today. Similarly, if Wang Jianlin ever gave up when he didn't even have enough food to eat, Wanda would never be such a phenomenal success story as a world-class company.

Sa: Speaking of persevering with our dreams, I believe everyone has his own judgment. However, young generations today face different problems and challenges including the probability of setbacks. How many of them are still willing to pursue their dreams? How long will they keep their dreams alive? And what attitudes do they have in terms of persevering with their dreams? What is more important for young people is that you need to know what is the dream that you really cherish in your heart and stick to it. For example, the majority of your classmates may choose to stay in big cities and find a decent job. Do you think that you should follow suit? What is the dream that you really cherish in your heart? Once you know this and persevere with your dreams, it's definitely worth it.

Wang Jianlin: The most important thing is that the career you choose should be something you enjoy doing yourself. Never choose something that you don't like and you're unsure of just for the sake of starting a successful business. You need to choose something that you really love and believe in its success from the bottom of your heart. My favorite catchphrase is: the most successful entrepreneurs are maniacs.

Li Shaobo: Nice to meet you, Mr. Wang. I'm from Fudan University. You once bet with Jack Ma (founder of Alibaba) that e-commerce wouldn't take up more than 50% of the Chinese retail market in ten years. If it did, you would pay him 100 million yuan, and otherwise he'd pay you the same amount. My question is why did you make the bet? And are you still convinced that you will win it?

Wang Jianlin: No. It was just a half joking bet, just between the two of us.

Sa: Half joking and half serious?

Wang Jianlin: Half serious. As for e-commerce, it's hard to tell who will win the bet after ten years. I was just expressing my opinion. No matter how successful his e-commerce stores become, they won't be able to replace physical stores. Additionally, consumer behavior… there's a type…we study consumer psychology, a significant proportion of purchases are driven by conspicuous consumption. Why do the girls want a certain handbag so badly? Why are public places the favorite hangout of fashionable girls and boys? They want to be the center of attention.

Sa: Right. Nobody can see them if they buy things on Taobao.

Wang Jianlin: So I said it's hard to tell ahead of time. I admit that I'm not sure about the scale of e-commerce in ten years.

Li Shaobo: Does it mean that back in 2012 you were totally confident of the bet, and now, knowing that you're about to lose the bet, you'll deny ever making it?

Wang Jianlin: No, no, no…If I lose when 2022 comes, I'll pay Jack Ma 100 million. It doesn't matter. I can't break my word, right?

Sa: Whose side are you on?

Li Shaobo: I'm on Ma's side, because I think informatization and the Internet are definitely the trends that are moving forward, and there's been a growing shift in people's buying habits toward the Internet… this is already a foregone conclusion.

Sa: But I'm really serious about it. You just said that the bet was made half jokingly and half seriously. I'm curious which half of it is a joke, and how much of it is serious? Is the 100 million part just a joke, or is it a serious bet?

Wang Jianlin: The 100 million bet is only half joking, but our debate about the e-commerce model is serious.

Xu Shengming: Hi, brother Wang. I enjoyed your speech very much. You said that a bold and thick-skinned approach is what it took for Wanda to be a success story across the country, and I really admire your ambitions.

Wang Jianlin: As I recall, I didn't say it quite like that. The meaning of what I said is that innovation is bold and experimenting and pioneering are daring. What I meant by a thick-skinned approach is that you must not be afraid when you first start a business…if you're too thin-skinned and dare not ask for help or advice…how can you possibly succeed in your business venture?

Xu Shengming: Then didn't you say something along the lines of (a degree from) Tsinghua or Peking university does not help as much as bold action?

Wang Jianlin: Yes, I did. I said (a degree from) Tsinghua or Peking university wouldn't help as much as a bold heart, meaning that regardless of your academic credentials and theoretical capability, you can never create a successful business if you're not daring and enterprising enough.

Xu Shengming: Your theory that a Tsinghua or Peking university degree doesn't help as much as bold action is what inspires me the most because I'm the only student among the eight of us here who's not from a top-ranking university, but I think that, like Sa, I've been bold and thick-skinned ever since I was a little boy. I'm always into new stuff and enjoy challenges…I always tell my competitors before every competition that I'll be the winner.

Wang Jianlin: So do you win?

Xu Shengming: Sometimes I win and sometimes I lose, of course. I personally think that youth is meant to be arrogant. Otherwise, it's not real youth. Would you agree?

Wang Jianlin: Young people shouldn't have any burdens. This is how outstanding talents emerge from among the rest. I agree with you very much on this.

Xu Shengming: My second question is do you still remember what is the most arrongant thing you said when you were young?

Wang Jianlin: The most arrogant thing…I tell you when I was a teenager before joining the army, I climbed a tree. Nobody dared to climb it, so I decided to do it…I fell off and broke my arm. And once, there was a rail…people jumped over it. I saw classmates two or three years my senior jump across the rail, but no one on this side dared to. I jumped, stumbled on the rail and fell down, broke this arm again.

Sa: But you broke the same arm in both incidents.

Wang Jianlin: Yes. Oddly enough, it was always this arm that I broke.

Sa: Such a poor arm.

Wang Jianlin: Let me give you a suggestion…arrogance and pride are different. I'd say pride is more appropriate…ambitious and with a strong sense of pride, but without being rude.

Xu Shengming: By arrongance, what I meant was confidence, recognition of one's own ability. Whatever we do, we need to do it following Mr. Wang's example – even after breaking an arm, he didn't stop climbing…Let's continue after the broken aarm has recovered and keep climbing until we reach the top of the highest mountain.

Sa: Mr. Wang Jianlin summarized it very well. That is, being proud. If you're truly talented and have solid competence, your sense of pride and enterprising spirit will bring you bright prospects. Thank you. Next, Gao Jiahan, please.

Gao Jiahan: Nice to meet you, Mr. Wang. During your speech just now and on many other occasions, you stressed the importance of innovation for Wanda. We all know that enterprises relying on innovation are typically characterized by a liberal and relaxed corporate culture, but wild rumors abound that you have an almighty existence in Wanda, rule everything there, and you're very strict with your employees. Female employees are not allowed to wear more than three pieces of jewelry, and two earrings are counted as two pieces. So I was curious as to how they could innovate in such a strict company? Is every innovation in Wanda created by Wang Jianlin alone?

Wang Jianlin: First, let me ask you a question: do you be- lieve "wild rumors?" The rumors are false in the first place. Actually, we have an employee handbook that requires or refers to etiquette requirements. Men must wear formal suits…it's one of the rules, a suit and tie. Girls must wear business attire. Moreover, you can see our innovations are not only limited to real estate but now also include culture, including tourism. These are all innovations. Many of them are not developed by colleagues or me but by foreigners. If all innovations came from me alone, I would've been exhausted to death years ago. That is impossible. The rumors can't be trusted.

Sa: Now that Mr. Wang has made it clear, all Wanda's female employees are spreading the news with tearful eyes…let's bring out our jewelry now.

Gao Jiahan: OK then. I've got another question that is also related to your company's management style. That is, your company organizes a journey of conscience every year, where the employees choose a village to visit the poor and ask about their sufferings…give donations. But the donations are made by the employees themselves and the company doesn't pay anything. I feel that the employees have the right to donate or choose not to. Doesn't it mean that you're using their money to earn a good reputation for your company?

Wang Jianlin: Our charitable donations mostly come from the company, but the reason why we made it a rule that the employees must visit poor families every year is that our company has developed rapidly and most of our businesses are operated in big cities. The employees have bought their own apartments and cars, and have a very decent income. Over time many of us become swollen-headed, and our frame of reference and coordinates of life change. They regard money as the only measurement of success. Hence, we started a campaign ten years ago, requiring every company to select one of the poorest local villages and visit every year. Donation is not mandatory. We call it Wanda volunteers. If you think the campaign has a major impact, it's not necessarily the case, but it works in a subtle and imperceptible way. Charity at Wanda... I don't want to see that it becomes a cause for me alone. Instead, it should be a culture, a cultural atmosphere within the company...an atmosphere of a positive attitude.

Gao Jiahan: OK. Thank you very much!

Sa: So for Mr. Wang now, the biggest problem is no longer how to make money but rather how to spend money, to help more people. This might be what he needs to consider in the future.

Wang Jianlin: I've declared a long time ago that I won't leave a big share of my wealth to my children.

Sa: Yes.

Wang Jianlin: As the ancient Chinese saying goes: if the son is not as good as the father, why bother to leave him an inheritance? If the son is better than the father, why bother to leave him an inheritance? That's it.

Ren Yufeng: Hi, Mr. Wang. I'm an entrepreneur.

Sa: What do you do exactly? What kind of business?

Ren Yufeng: I'm in the catering business, running a chain restaurant.

Sa: Is it dandan mian (a type of spicy noodle from Sichuan)?

Ren Yufeng: No, our specialties are Taiwanese snacks. I have two restaurants, so it's a traditional industry, and what you're doing now can also be categorized as a traditional business. In your opinion, how can we keep innovating and transcending ourselves within traditional industries?

Wang Jianlin: I don't really agree with such a categorization. Instead, I think the business you're in is a promising one.

Sa: Food is the paramount necessity of the people.

Wang Jianlin: Food is the paramount necessity of the people, and catering is characterized as an industry by repeated consumption. As the owner of a restaurant chain, you need to learn how to standardize.

Sa: It's hardly scalable.

Wang Jianlin: There's one cook…if there are ten cooks in a restaurant, maybe only two of them are really good. Whatever they make tastes good, but dishes made by the others taste different. You're running a chain, so how do you guarantee (quality) when you have 100 cooks? Hence, the most important thing is to improve the cost-performance ratio. Your products should either taste better than others' while offering the same price, or be priced lower while offering the same taste. Talent is more important. For example, if you have five buddies running the business together, I believe it will be a success.

Sa: That's why I think of all the eight representatives, you benefit the most from the show today. Not only did you talk face-to-face with Mr. Wang, but had the remarks he just made. You tell me, how many entrepreneurs in China can ask Mr. Wang to give some suggestions face-to-face?

Sa: Today, Mr. Wang Jianlin shared with us his life story from his teenage years all the way through successes and, of course, setbacks. His story won't be repeated exactly by any one of us, but there are certain things that we all need to adhere to, such as his personality, honesty, integrity, perseverance and creativity. Let's have another round of applause for Mr. Wang's inspiring speech! Thank you!

Wang Jianlin: Thank you!

Chapter Two

Determination

Where There's a Will, There's a Way

22 June, 2013 – A Speech at Huashang College

In June 2013, Huashang College held the first (Summer) Finance and Investment Forum in which Wang Jianlin gave a speech to over 2,000 college students from across China. During the speech, he talked about his personal experience of starting Wanda under huge debt burdens and financial difficulties, expounding on the entrepreneurial philosophy of "where there's a will, there's a way".

Here's his speech:

Hello everyone, good afternoon!

It's my honor to be here today to share with you my experience as a businessman, at the request of Professor Liu Jipeng. It's my first time to Huashang College, and I'm deeply impressed to know that the college has so many courses, with an extensive alumni network throughout the country. As the old saying goes: 'every subject has its own experts, and every trade has its masters.'

I'm not sure what I should talk about during my first visit here. I understand that students in Huashang College are mostly from private enterprises, and the majority are small and medium sized businesses. During forums I attended in the past, I usually talked about Wanda's business model and corporate culture, but these are relevant only to large enterprises. I want my speech to be useful for the students here. So what should I talk about? I kept thinking about it over and over again and decided to share with you my insights about successful business management. I'd like to entitle my speech "Where there's a will, there's a way." I don't like reading scripts, so I'll speak for 30 minutes and will allow some time for questions and answers. You may send your questions to the host or ask questions yourself. There's no restriction whatsoever. Anything can be asked.

Four aspects of the theme "where there's a will, there's a way" will be discussed.

First, small companies can become large enterprises. You may be running an enterprise with an annual revenue of several millions or tens of millions of yuan. Then, will your company remain a small enterprise forever? And are the large enterprises born to be large ones? No. All the big multinationals in the world are developed from small companies. We all know that Bill Gates – the richest man in the world – founded Microsoft. Gates decided to start his own business and started it up in a small lab in a garage. He only had US$3,000 at first, but now he's the richest man in the entire world with an annual income of tens of billions of dollars every year.

Li Ka-shing, the richest Chinese, has HK$200 billion worth of assets and ranks among the richest men in the world. He owns such a big company, but it was a producer of plastic flowers at first. Those of you at a younger age may not know that back in the 1960s, plastic flowers were very popular. At that time, it was impossible to have real flowers in houses, and when needed, people used plastic to make flowers. It was very small in those years and made tens of thousands of Hong Kong dollars per year.

Now, take my company as an example. Wanda Group is pretty big today. Our total assets are estimated to exceed 350 billion yuan this year, and were over 300 billion yuan last year. This year, it'll grow to at least 350 billion yuan. We will pay almost 30 billion yuan in taxes this year. The figure was over 200 billion yuan last year. Our after-tax profit margin will be nearly 10%. In addition to revenue, Wanda has ranked No.

1 among all private enterprises across all other indicators such as assets, profit and taxes throughout the past several years. How did we grow? We borrowed one million yuan in 1988. Back then the minimum registered capital required for real estate companies was one million yuan. We didn't have 1 million, so we found a state-owned enterprise, a very rich state-owned enterprise at that time, and borrowed one million yuan from them. However, they told us that we needed to provide a guarantor, and it (the guarantor) took half of it straight away, only giving us the remaining half million. We couldn't say no! After 25 years, the company has now grown into a large enterprise. Our revenue increased rapidly. In particular, despite widespread difficulties in 2012, we managed to maintain a growth rate of 34.8%, and it is projected to be over 30% this year.

Our objective is to slow down the revenue growth slightly from the current rate and hit 350 billion yuan in 2015 and maintain a 15% growth rate in the next several years. Our revenue will grow to US$100 billion by 2020, and we're well on track to rank among the top 100 largest companies in the world by that time in terms of assets, revenue and profit alike.

The company has developed at an amazing pace. How did we do it? We started as a small firm too. You know, all of the biggest enterprises in the world today are around 100 years old, so not that long. The oldest family business in Europe has gone into the seventh generation and lasted more than 200 years. No company in the world can sustain success for 200 or 300 years. One hundred years is the absolute limit. We always say century-old enterprises but not millennium-old enterprises. Why? It's unrealistic.

Less than 10% of Fortune Global 500 companies 50 years ago are still on the list today, and about 20% of those listed 10 years ago have disappeared. This may sound surprising to you.

Ten years ago, there were only seven Chinese companies listed as Fortune 500, and it increased to over 70 last year. Large enterprises emerged and died out. Why is this? Because were it not for this lifeand-death cycle of the enterprises and their "short-lived" nature, new generations of entrepreneurs wouldn't have been motivated to create great enterprises.

If enterprises all last 500 years or even longer, it would be demotivating for entrepreneurs, and enterprises would be reluctant to change.

Small enterprises can grow into large enterprises. What does this mean? Although your company is relatively small in size for now, it doesn't mean that it will stay small in the future. It can't be small and medium enterprises forever, and it may well become a large enterprise, a super enterprise. This all depends on how ambitious you are.

Second, all excellent enterprises have their unique DNA. It's unrealistic to assume that an enterprise can perform well only after it has accumulated 500 billion yuan or grown to a certain scale. I always say that excellent enterprises must have unique DNA. What's DNA? It's the genetic code of an enterprise, meaning that the enterprise is genetically built to grow into an excellent enterprise during its very conception. Here we hope that small and medium enterprises, most enterprises should have such ambition.

It's wrong to say that an enterprise can excel only after it has reached a certain large scale. I know a company. It specializes in producing gas- kets for nuclear weapons, which used to be a technology exclusively owned by the U.S. and imported gaskets were very expensive. The com- pany owner studied the technology carefully and decided to enter the business. He became successful after ten years of committed efforts. His products are recognized for their unrivalled sealing effect, outshining their U.S. counterparts. His factory is not big and earns 100-200 million yuan a year, but it plays a crucial role. Because it produces the gaskets, China no longer needs to import the central component. Due to the success of his enterprise, his American competitors offered to buy it for US$500 million. If the entrepreneur had chosen to trade it off for a comfortable life, it would be very simple – 500 million dollars are more than what he could possibly spend in his life – but he didn't sell the enterprise. He had even bigger plans and was determined to continue developing his enterprise in the business or other related industries. In recognition of his ambitious commitment and the highly specialized nature of his business, he received support from the government. I'm sure that his company will become an excellent enterprise in the future.

No matter how excellent an enterprise is, its excellence is not acquired after business scale-up, but "conceived" at birth. From the beginning, the entrepreneur must be ambitious and aspire to a great enterprise. It is such ambitions that drive him to success. They're written in the genes.

Third, aim high and you'll achieve more. There are different types of ambitions – big ones, medium ones and small ones. In other words, money can be made on three levels. At the lowest level, one gets rich and enjoys a happy life and family. There's nothing wrong with this. This is the mostly commonly heard ambition. We work hard to make life more comfortable for ourselves, our family and children. It's not a low-level thing in itself, but neither is it at a high level as an ambition. Hence, I call it the lowest level of money-making. At the second level, the aim is to create a large-scale business and make money…reap fame and wealth. In other words, the entrepreneur no longer runs a business and seeks wealth only for himself, but for spiritual enjoyment. He's interested in developing a large-scale, influential and respected enterprise. How to gain the respect of others? Generally speaking, influential large or super scale enterprises are more respected, making it easier for them to gather resources and grow.

Entrepreneurs should aspire to make their enterprises bigger, more influential and more respected. Instead of making money for ourselves, we should incorporate social responsibility into our business operations, making our enterprises part of the social wealth.

At the highest level of entrepreneurship, we develop enterprises at a spiritual level to satisfy our spiritual needs, to make our enterprises the pride of the country, the private sector and industry, or to establish our enterprises as market leaders in the world. This is a spiritual quest. To put it using the buzzword, we need to create excellent enterprises as corporate citizens, where the ultimate goal behind moneymaking is to repay society. At this level, we have more than enough money to spend. That's why most of the enterprises today who perform their corporate social responsibilities well, who donate a lot, do a lot of voluntary work or focus on specific charitable causes…most of them are large enterprises. This conforms to this theory.

Perhaps all of you here today have just started your enterprises or have been running your business for several years or ten years, but your enterprises remain relatively small in size. What aspirations should such enterprises have? In short, it's exactly as an advertisement puts it: your stage is as big as your heart. We must aim high.

Let me tell you a little story of myself when I first started Wanda. In 1989, I went to Hong Kong for the first time together with four friends. We stayed at the best hotel back then, "Grand Hyatt." It was inside the old Hong Kong Convention and Exhibition Center. There were four towers above the center, including Grand Hyatt, Seaview Hotel and an office building. There was an open terrace measuring around 20,000 square meters on the 11th floor of the four towers. It had a great atmosphere. There were two swimming pools for guests of the hotels to relax. We went there during the day and really loved it. We went there again in the evening. Back then, we felt Hong Kong was such a great place. I said it was an inspiring place. I would work as hard as I could to get a building like this in my life.

My friend Mr. Huang asked me whether I knew that it cost a lot of money, about HK$2 billion. I said although I had just started in the real estate business, and I didn't believe that I couldn't even own a building 20 or 30 years after my retirement. They laughed and thought it was just a joke. Wanda's annual profit was one million yuan, but I had the ambition and worked very hard to achieve it, which actually didn't take us very long and we built the first tower in 1993. It was a little smaller than that in Hong Kong. So how many towers built so far? We've opened 80 shopping malls and 50 five-star hotels. We hold 18 million square meters of properties, which will increase to about 22 million next year.

All the five largest real estate companies in the world are from the U.S. where land supplies are large and the population is big. Among them, the youngest is 80 years old, and the oldest has been in operation for over 100 years. Thanks to China's enormous territory and 8%-9% annual economic growth, we've been growing at a similar pace.

If I didn't have that ambition that day, perhaps Wanda wouldn't be such a success story today. Of course, there are many factors contributing to success, and ambition is just one of them. Ambition must be supplemented with other ingredients such as the correct direction, professionalism, talent, human resources and the ability to integrate social resources, etc., but being ambitious is the fundamental element. How big your ambitions are dictates how big your enterprise will become. If you only have ambitions at the lowest level, you can earn 200-300 million yuan in China to enjoy the rest of your life, as many entrepreneurs do. There's nothing wrong if an entrepreneur retires after making a few hundred million yuan, and many entrepreneurs have chosen to do so. Now that I've shared with you my theory of success, I hope that some of you here and more people can commit themselves to "big ambitions." Big ambitions give your enterprise the "genes" for big success and make big success possibilities.

What's the most important thing after you've set ambitions? Perseverance – the determination to work toward the preset goals despite difficulties, challenges, setbacks, criticisms, etc. Here, I have two examples to share with you.

At the end of 1992, when Wanda was still a small enterprise, I was entrusted by the government to develop a project in the downtown area. They tried to talk me into accepting the commission, but I found it too risky. However, for the sake of cooperation with the government, I accepted the old city transformation project under enormous pressure. These days, relocation compensation is paid in a lump sum. But it was different back then, and every household affected was only paid less than 10,000 yuan as the "transition" cost. There were more than 6,000 households in total. The project came to a halt after the first 4,000 households, because rectifications started.

A wave of government regulations came. I experienced seven government regulations during my 25-year career as a real estate developer. At first, it was called rectification and later changed to macro-level regulation. They're the same thing in essence. The one I'm talking about that occurred in 1992 was still called rectification. At that time, government regulation measures were much tougher. A document was distributed and all real estate related loans were suspended. All property developers were banned from taking out bank loans, not even a penny. Our company operated smoothly and progressed well with the large transformation project until the loan suspension. It left me in a tight corner and there was no way out. I didn't sleep at all for nine days. I tried everything but just couldn't go to sleep. I was on the verge of paranoid schizophrenia. I fainted during a meeting at the company. My colleagues sent me to the neurology department of the former Beijing Hospital. Luckily, the doctor said that he knew how to get me to sleep. Perhaps my body took the psychological hint, and I fell asleep the minute I took his medicine. It was all because of the loan suspension.

Leaders of the municipal government understood the company was facing after accepting the government project and came to my rescue. They told the manager of a state-owned bank to grant me a loan of 20 million yuan. Back then, Wanda's annual revenue was 700-800 million yuan, and it was no longer a small company. However, in order to secure the loan...perhaps the bank manager did not want to give me the loan, or there were some government-related reasons, he told me to come back in five days. I did but it didn't work out, and it went on this way several times. In the end, I went to his office more than 50 times. I couldn't break in without permission, so I had to wait outside. Sometimes literally all day long, but I just couldn't see him.

Just think about it: as a business owner, I waited outside the bank manager's office all day long...for days in a row. To develop Wanda into a large enterprise, I've experienced setbacks even worse than this.

And this is why I submitted several proposals as a member of the CPPCC (the Chinese People's Political Consultative Conference, a political advisory body in China) appealing for a solution to the financing difficulties small businesses face. I've gone through it myself.

If the funding problem can be effectively addressed, private enterprises will be able to develop at a more rapid pace, much faster than state-owned enterprises (SOEs). Seventy percent of financial capital is occupied by SOEs, but they do not offer sufficient employment opportunities. In terms of jobs, SOEs account for 13%, and private enterprises 87%. The latter also contribute over 90% of new employment opportunities every year. In terms of taxes, President XiJinping said during a meeting with private enterprise representatives in 2013 that private enterprises contributed more than half of China's total tax revenue.

Were it not for our firm commitment to our aspirations, the company would have already died a long time ago. When we were small we had two big problems. The first problem is to do with land purchase. An office chief of the government planning department. If he wants to see you, you must act immediately and visit him straight away. Otherwise, you won't be able to see him. What's more, you have to wait outside sometimes for several days, which has happened to me many times in the past. It was exactly because of these setbacks that we decided to set ambitious aspirations. We must develop a unique "Wanda model" and keep improving the company so that we no longer need to ask for the help from others, but people come to us for help instead.

Humiliations like this and the financing difficulties strengthened my determination to scale up my company, and to develop a business model that makes people come to us for help. As we developed over the years…as I just mentioned, Wanda became the second-largest real estate developer in the world, and the Wanda model has gained in popularity worldwide. Today, all of our development projects are conducted on an invitation basis. That is, if there are 100 people inviting us to develop properties, we only choose 50. From 2008 onward, we launched a new business model shifting toward the cultural and tourism industries.

We established Wanda Culture Industry Group last year. It became the largest cultural enterprise and posted 20.8 billion yuan of revenue in its first year of operation. According to the top 50 global cultural companies list released by a well-known European advisory company, we ranked No. 38. We believe that Wanda Culture Group will make it to the top 20 in 2015 or 2016, and grow into one of the world's top10 cultural enterprises by 2020. Why did we decide to enter the cultural industry? We need to create stronger competitive advantages, with higher entry barriers and specialization…a business that requires creativity and special talent. After all, we want people to come to us and ask for help. This way, the company will be respected rather than humiliated. For any small enterprise, once it becomes highly specialized in a certain business, as I said, a company that has developed a product with core competitiveness will be respected by others although its annual revenue may only be 50-60 million yuan.

Given the time constraints, I only talked about my personal experience of business development to illustrate the topic: the success of an enterprise depends on a combination of factors, but the most important one is to set up "ambitious aspirations" for the enterprise and encode these into its corporate "DNA" – your stage is as big as your heart. Thank you!

Q&A

Q: Why can Wanda always secure land at prime locations at excellent prices, but we can't?

Wang Jianlin: I've already talked about this issue. Indeed, some real estate developers argued that Wanda acquired land at good locations across the country. It's true that our land prices are cheap, but we rarely purchase land within central business districts. Instead, we typically go to places that most competitors dare not enter. Years ago, land of the Shijingshan and Babaoshanin districts of Beijing was offered by the government, and the government asked us to develop a business center. No other companies were interested. They say that there's no business outside the second west ring road, and the land is actually located outside the fourth ring road. Who dares to go there? We're totally confident in our business model. We usually go to places that conform to the general urban development trend, or fully developed areas where business facilities are lacking. Firstly, this caters to the development needs of the government and the local communities. Secondly, Wanda's business model, it would be an overstatement to say that only we can do the business, but we're confident that we can do it better. Wanda's core competitive strength is our speed – within our projects, all businesses are open in less than two years or typically within 1.5 years to be more precise.

Due to our core competitiveness, when we're invited to develop a project, we have the bargaining power, regardless of whether the inviter is a government department or a company. Therefore, we can ask for 1,000 yuan when the offer is 2,000. If the proposed cut is accepted, we can start the project straight away, and otherwise we can take our time and negotiate with the inviter, since we've got plenty of other projects to work on. As I mentioned just now, why can we purchase land at relatively low prices? Competitiveness is the main reason. When you have a trump card, meet the conditions for negotiation and have the bargaining power, it's only natural that you'll get land at relatively low costs.

Q: I have three questions: Can Wanda continue to be successful without Wang Jianlin? How are business-government relations handled at Wanda? What's your approach to wealth inheritance?

Wang Jianlin: Can Wanda be successful without Wang Jianlin? I can tell you for sure, yes, Wanda can do without me. Why? Because even though I've stayed in the company my entire life, I'll die one day. No one can change this. So I can leave Wanda, but it's only a matter of time. We set it to be 2020. By retirement I meant stepping down as the chairman rather than CEO. I've not worked as the CEO for many years.

I said seven or eight years ago that I'd retire when Wanda hits the 100 billion yuan threshold. Back then, I felt that it would take 10 or 20 years for the company to realize annual revenue of 100 billion yuan– it was only 10 billion at that time. My colleagues asked me would I retire after the company hits 100 billion. I said the target set was too low. So I reset it to be 2020, when I'll step down as chairman.

Second, how to effectively handle business-government relations in China? This is something no one can get around when doing business in China. I once recommended that businessmen should "stay close with the government but away from politics." Many people argued that I can keep the government away from my business. Actually, even if you were in the U.S. or the UK, you'd still find it impossible to run a business without keeping abreast of the latest government policies, etc. Given the government-dominated nature of the Chinese economy, businessmen here cannot work around the government, and this is particularly true for real estate developers. The best way of keeping normal business-government relations is to develop a business where the government has to come to you for help. Our businesses are all conducted on an invitation basis, and this makes things much easier. These days, wherever our development team goes, they're wined and dined by our business partners. It's that simple. One of the benefits of this is that they can drink like a fish now.

Third, wealth inheritance. I think wealth inheritance shouldn't be interpreted within the context of traditional Chinese culture. Inheritance is not necessarily limited to family members. I'm very open-minded. Wanda currently has 100,000 employees, and this will grow to 200,000-300,000 by 2020, when our annual revenue is expected to increase to US$100 billion. The company will not necessarily be inherited by my child. If he's qualified for it, he can inherit the company of course. But what if he's not suitable for it? It's not a good thing either for the child or for the enterprise. As the ancient Chinese saying goes: 'If the son is not as good as the father, why bother to leave him an inheritance? If the son is better than the father, why bother to leave him an inheritance?' I'll wait and see. I still have eight years. If my son proves himself competent to inherit the business, I'd be happy to see that happen. If not, I'll choose professional managers, with my son acting as the major shareholder. My son is a very ambitious man and wants to start his own business. He even said that as his company gets bigger, he'll acquire Wanda Group.

Q: How do you ensure that every partner involved in Wanda projects has equal opportunities for cooperation?

Wang Jianlin: This question should be answered for two types of partners, i.e. constructors and tenants.

In terms of construction operations, we laid down a rule ten years ago that for all construction projects, Wanda only cooperates with China State Construction Engineering Corporation (China State Construction) to ensure smooth cooperation. Our construction partners today are mainly the first, second, fourth and eighth divisions of China State Construction, the reason being only strategic cooperation can ensure quality and prevent bribery. We're willing to maintain long-term cooperation with the company, and China State Construction receives a large proportion (a third or more) of its business from us. This way, it always attaches great importance to Wanda projects and can make sacrifices for our projects when necessary. In addition, such a cooperation model eliminates bribery for the most part and ensures quality construction.

To be honest with you, the most important competitive advantage of Wanda today is not capital, human resources or our business model, but rather our business resources. At present, we have signed cooperation agreements with more than 5,000 tenants, over 300 of which were overseas. In each project, we select the tenants rather than attract them. For specific businesses, we can't guarantee that our tenant team allocates among the candidates in an absolutely fair and impartial manner, but we strive to be impartial in everything we do. We have established brand pools for catering, entertainment, gym and closing businesses. Retailers applying to enter the brand pools must meet certain criteria such as the length of business operation, the number of stores opened and so on.

Generally speaking, all retailers that have excellent products and properly qualified construction companies have the opportunity to cooperate with Wanda. We seek to achieve mutual growth with our partners. I never perceive Wanda as "Party A." Instead, we focus on common development and respect our construction contractors and tenants. Our tenant conference is held every year. I attend each conference in person and meet hundreds of interested retailers. Some of them are limited in size and don't need to be visited in person, but I want to remind my colleagues by example that all of our partners and tenants should be respected, regardless of their size.

Q: Please advise how we can rent a shop in Wanda Plaza, and will any discounts be offered for Huashang students?

Wang Jianlin: Unfortunately, Wanda sets itself apart, first and foremost, by impartial business management, which involves management regulations, planning and information. Business management is our greatest strength. Because of my military origin, I place great emphasis on management rules. We developed different regulations for every industry and department, and the regulations are highly practical and quantified wherever possible. The requirements are simplified to the greatest extent, and therefore can be easily applied. Secondly, complete planning is carried out before the launch of every single project and tenant attraction campaign. Thirdly, all plans are entered into the information center module.

To be honest, corruption is a widespread issue in construction and commerce, and Wanda is no exception, so I do my best to standardize our actions through regulations. Therefore, my answer to this question is that I can't break the rules for Huashang students. No discounts, sorry.

Q: Where will the Chinese real estate industry go in the next ten years? Will the government offer support through public finance? Will the housing prices fall? Will there be a day when we can't afford to buy a home?

Wang Jianlin: The development trend of the real estate industry... one thing's for sure, you can ask me again after 15 years. There won't be any major issues or systemic risks for the Chinese real estate market. A crash won't happen. This is mainly because urbanization and industrialization have not yet been completed in China. First, urbanization. Fifty-two percent of the Chinese population lives in urban areas, but the actual urbanization rate is below 40%. Of the people living in Chinese cities, 250 million of them don't have urban residence account (household registration) and are not entitled to local social security benefits. The real urbanization should start with the "urbanization of people" – that is, turning migrants into "urban people." In view of this, the government plans an increase of one percentage point every year, meaning that 14 million people will be added to China's urban population every year. Judging by the experiences of other countries, the urbanization process won't slow down until it reaches 80%, by which time the real estate market will start to contract. The urbanization rate in China is 52%, which is well below 80%, or the minimum threshold of 70%, so we still have 18 percentage points to go, corresponding to 200 million people.

In addition, industrialization has not been completed either. China's steel output is 6-7 billion tons per year, less than 8 billion tons. Upon completion of industrialization, steel output needs to reach 15-20 billion tons. In this respect, the real estate industry will keep growing overall without systemic risks during the next 15 years, but local risks may emerge. It's up to individual consumers to decide the extent of the risks involved. The larger a city is, the less risks are involved, and vice-versa.

Q: A company wants to pay you to endorse their product. How much would you charge?

Wang Jianlin: Sorry, I'm no longer a young boy, and nor am I any hot girl. It sounds totally irrelevant. If you have a serious business proposition, you may fax it and write me down as the recipient. We can see if cooperation is feasible. I'm not the first to read incoming faxes and mails, as we get tons of donation requests every day. They'll sort the correspondence for me first. You fax your proposition and my fax number can be found online.

Q: One of the students here has started his own business. He wants to talk with you and is willing to pay you 50% earnings in return. Would you meet him?

Wang Jianlin: He doesn't need to pay me a penny. I can talk with him and offer some suggestions. He may make an appointment with my assistant.

Q: How will the yachting industry develop in China, in your opinion? Why did you decide to acquire a foreign yacht producer?

Wang Jianlin: There are over 1,000 yacht producers worldwide. The most famous two are from Italy and the UK, and their products are dubbed "Bentley and Rolls Royce on water." There are two reasons. First, airplanes and yachts are the biggest luxury goods. It takes 80-100 years for any luxury brand to establish itself. Once established, it becomes a valuable asset to acquire. Second, the acquisition was also borne out of business considerations. We're making investments in cultural tourism sites in Qingdao and Sanya. The local governments require that each site be equipped with yachts. Compared with purchasing a dozen boats for each site, it's a better deal to acquire the producer. Additionally, I'm bullish about the development of yachts and private jets in China going forward. Yachts and jets are both high-frequency luxury goods, for which the import tariff is set at 45%. If they can be produced in China, tax savings alone will give us a significant competitive edge.

Q: I heard you made a bet with Jack Ma, so who will win in 10 years?

Wang Jianlin: I've been asked about this over and over again ever since last year. To be honest, the bet was made purely at the request of China Central Television (CCTV). Jack and I teamed up as presenters of the annual CCTV economic awards. The director said we needed to inject humor into the event. How could we do that? We made a bet. This was the most important reason for the bet. It was more like a joke.

Secondly, Jack and I…we needed to play for and against in the debate. He represented the Internet, and I had to represent traditional industries and commerce, and I was playing my role to defend the idea that traditional businesses still had plenty of room for further growth. As to who the winner will be, I can't tell. If I say I'll win, Jack won't be happy to hear that. If I say he'll win, it'll make me feel bad.

Q: How will commercial property and health-related property develop in the future?

Wang Jianlin: At present, health-related properties are actually grouped under the category of holiday-tourism real estate. The state will push forward housing properties for senior citizens. I'd say senior citizen housing property represents better opportunities than health. Most of us still don't have a clear understanding of senior-citizen housing properties. Wanda got too involved and tied up with commercial properties and cultural businesses, and I considered entering the senior-citizen housing property market three years ago. Going forward, the retirement industry will certainly become a major industry in China in five to 10 years, by which time 20% of the national population will be aged above 60. Related businesses will have an enormous market. Furthermore, land may be purchased for developing senior housing properties by directly signing an agreement, and this is also supported by tax incentives. By converting health properties to elderly housing properties, you may even secure the land directly by signing an agreement without public bidding.

Q: Wanda stepped up deployment of its commercial property model in response to the "Chinese Dream." How's the Hong Kong IPO (initial public offering) progressing for Wanda?

Wang Jianlin: Wanda has not been listed so far, and this makes many people curious. I'm always convinced that Wanda will be listed, especially my core assets including culture. I missed out on a good opportunity. Previously I could have listed the company in Hong Kong, but I was fooled by an Australian investment bank called Macquarie. They advised me not to launch an IPO and set up a trust fund instead; and then I could establish a management company to control the entire group. I followed their advice and abandoned the IPO, and set up a trust fund, but this was totally new in the Hong Kong market. The CSRC (China Securities Regulatory Commission) insisted that the first company must be a local company based in Hong Kong, and companies from outside wouldn't be approved. As a result, it took me over one year to list the Link REITs (Real Estate Investment Trusts) in Hong Kong. Tough luck – the state then banned this for private enterprises after the fund was listed, so I had to apply for an IPO again, but government regulation was in full swing all these years. Therefore, we're considering different listing models, while taking into account the latest market conditions. One thing's for sure – Wanda will be listed in the near future, and various financial data and development information will be made available.

Q: Please tell us your opinion about football. How much does Wanda football team invest each year?

Wang Jianlin: My opinion about football? None in particular. Investment per year is 200 million yuan, 600 million in three years. I'm a supporter of Chinese football. I ran a club before but no more now; I've gotten out of it entirely. The government leaders care about it very much, and the Chinese administration of sports made several appeals, so I came back and am offering support for Chinese football. Despite the recent 5-1 loss to Thailand, the Chinese football market is healthy overall. The Chinese team used to be a leader in Asia. We once beat Japan 2-0. In those days, only South Korea was a strong opponent of China, but the number of opponents has increased in recent years. Many times we advised relevant government departments to look further ahead than immediate results. More attention should be attached to young players, and China's football can be improved only if the number of young players can be increased. For example, the total population of South Korea is only 40 million, but it has 600,000-700,000 registered teenage players. By contrast, there were only 10,000 registered players out of 1.3 billion Chinese people, corresponding to one registered player every 10,000 people. When I invested in football, there were 400,000 young players in China. There's been such a dramatic decline. It will be difficult for Chinese football to improve unless the number of young players is increased.

Back then, the Chinese team had HaoHaidong (a famous soccer player in China). He was very fast and could run 100 meters in 11 seconds. Is there anyone in the Chinese team now who can run as fast and play as well?

If we're really serious about developing football in China, we can't focus on immediate results. The Chinese football will certainly improve if we have one million teenage players.

Q: How was financing carried out at Wanda during different stages?

Wang Jianlin: Financing at different stages. I just told my story... it used to be a headache before. We had to do whatever it took for the sake of the company. Today, Wanda is a major client at the head offices of the four state-owned banks, and financing has become easier.

I'm not representative of private enterprises here. Financing is still very difficult for them.

Q: My question is representative of most students here. If I want to enter the real estate market, could you give me some suggestions?

Wang Jianlin: You should have done it before. The real estate industry is suffering from overcapacity. If you really want to enter this business, don't go to housing property. Land purchase for housing property development is now conducted purely through auction. If you bid 100 million yuan, your competitor will offer 200 million yuan. You stand little chance of winning the bid. If you enter now, don't touch pure housing properties, commercial, industrial or tourism properties, but senior citizen housing property may be a good idea, because listing and bidding are not required. My suggestion is to stay away from the real estate industry, as small enterprises are increasingly deprived of opportunities. Why has the number of real estate developers been reduced to eight? Because almost all land resources have been acquired, leaving little opportunity for others.

I've enjoyed meeting and talking with you here for the past two hours. It's my first time to this forum. Because of my tight schedule and time constraints, I only talked about my personal experiences and stories. What I said is not a textbook or preaching. I just wanted us to be able to share our real thoughts with each other.

Chapter Three

Execution

Decoding the Execution of Wanda Group

12 April, 2014 – Speech at China Europe International Business School

I've delivered many speeches in recent years on topics ranging from Wanda's corporate strategy to corporate culture and from transformation and upgrade to tourism. Most of you are entrepreneurs. Today, I'd like to talk about our execution from the perspective of corporate management and I hope everyone present here can carry something away.

Wanda has been widely recognized for its strong execution these years. It has maintained unprecedented growth of more than 30% for eight consecutive years – with the fastest annual growth at 45%. We have never pushed back our scheduled opening dates for Wanda Plaza projects, and all these projects have been completed within a tight timeframe. I want to take this opportunity to share with you how Wanda develops such strong execution, focusing on four aspects:

I. Strong Execution

Our strong execution is mainly reflected in two aspects:

First, keeping our promise. When we start construction on any project – be it plazas, hotels, shopping malls or cinemas – we set the day they will become operational. Every September, Wanda holds a business conference – a premier event in the Chinese business calendar – that is attended by over 10,000 people, of which over 1,000 are business people. At that conference, we announce the specific opening dates for all Wanda Plaza and hotel projects for the next year. You may find it strange that we make the specific opening dates public one year in advance. Isn't this just asking for trouble? Actually, we do so because we consider the interests of business people: for our tenants, whether we open on May 1, October 1 or during the lunar New Year makes a world of a difference in terms of recruiting staff, preparing merchandise, etc. Also the sales volume in a peak season does not compare with that of a low season. Profits in the commercial sector are thin. Imagine we promised our tenants an opening on May 1. They would start to hire staff, stock their inventories, etc. Then, come May 1, imagine if we said, "Sorry, we won't be operational until October 1 or New Year's Day." Their stock would sit in storage, unable to be sold. And even if the losses from unsold merchandise were still manageable, think about half-a-year's worth of wages. That would eat away much of the future profits.

Many years ago, Wanda came up with the slogan: "allow businesses to make money," and the punctual start of operations is a crucial aspect in that commitment. We have been in the commercial property sector for 15 years and have practically never postponed the opening date for any project. What's more, when a Wanda Plaza opens for business, it means every single business is ready. Not a few dozen out of 200 or 300.

Second, maintaining costs below estimate. In real estate development, controlling costs is tough. First, there is a long development horizon. Unlike a car that can be assembled in minutes, a shopping mall may take Wanda two or three years between the groundbreaking and start of operations. Many companies may need four or five years. And the longer the time, the more variables are involved. Second, real estate is created in non-standard ways. Depending on the region, a mall is constructed differently. The type of tenant is not the same. What sells well in northern China may move off the store shelves less quickly in southern China. As a result, it is normal for many developers that the actual expenditure is 15-20% more than what has been budgeted, but for the over 100 real estate projects that Wanda has developed in the last 15 years, no matter whether these were malls or hotels, all achieved below-estimate costs and above-estimate net profit. That is what sets us apart from other developers.

We have built two mega cultural projects in Wuhan, including the Han Show Theatre and the Wanda Movie Park that cost 2.5 billion and 3.5 billion yuan, respectively. These projects will be open for business in the fourth quarter. Characterized by sophisticated design and technical complexity, the Han Show Theatre and Wanda Movie Park have charted our future direction for project development in the cultural sector. While building these groundbreaking projects, we've come up with many ideas and tried them out. The projects have taken more than five years since construction started in 2009. They are scheduled to be completed and delivered on June 20. All the costs are currently within budget. Wanda's strong cost control is demonstrated by lower-than-expected costs for such groundbreaking and high-tech cultural projects as the Han Show Theatre and Wanda Movie Park.

II. Create a Culture of Execution

Wanda's strong execution stems from the group-wide culture of execution. The concept of execution is in the blood of each employee at Wanda:

1. Lead by example

It seems to me that top management at a majority of private companies, SOEs and even government officials are not confident enough to lead by example in everything they do, but it is a principle that I've been living by for years, which may be inherited from my military background. At Wanda, I translate the principle into practice and act as a role model who leads by example for my employees. For example, nepotism is disallowed in the group as part of our anti-corruption campaign. I act in strict accordance with the rule and never have any relatives working with the group. I may give them money to set up a business on their own, but they are not allowed to join Wanda. It is by no means easy to walk the talk. Talents with a global mind-set are warmly welcomed by

Wanda on its way to becoming a world-leading company. I don't want people to think of Wanda as a family business, where the boss has the final say in all matters and the decision-making process lacks transparency. If Wanda were such a company, it would struggle to become international. As an absolute majority shareholder of Wanda, I've never had my expenses reimbursed at the group as part of my commitment not to hurt the interests of minority shareholders.

2. Nothing is impossible

At Wanda, no one would claim that a target set through the process of deliberation could not be met. Of course, the targets formulated by Wanda are scientific and realistic. We spend three months every year establishing plans for the next year. Business lines propose their respective plans every September, and after three months of discussions and deliberations among relevant stakeholders, the board of directors has the final say about which plans are the best. Everyone thinks of ways to complete the task. I have never heard of people making up excuses for failing to complete a task. This goes back to something that I have said all along: when you want to achieve something, you will always find a way. When you don't want to achieve something, you can always find excuses. Completing a task not only benefits your take-home pay, it is also a matter of pride. Every year, a ranking is carried out by the group for all projects completed the same year, like malls and hotels based on their quality, and the result will be announced on a big display board outside the venue of the group's annual outing. Those lowest-ranked general managers will be under enormous pressure and feel ashamed in front of their team members. It leaves these managers no choice but to try harder to keep pace with or even exceed others. This sort of corporate culture is so engrained at Wanda that not completing a task well will be felt as a humiliation by every Wanda employee.

Wanda has started its first project in Guangzhou – Baiyun Wanda Plaza. It has a total floor area of more than 400,000 square meters, two basement levels and more than ten floors. It was built and opened in just 11 months as compared to the originally planned two years, as we agreed to a call by the local municipal government to open the plaza to the public before the Asian Games were held in the city. Without our strong execution culture and capabilities, it would have been impossible for us to greatly shorten the development cycle of the project as required by the local government. This project represents a record in terms of the speed of project development in the world's commercial and architectural history. The plaza was a complete success despite being built in such a short time frame. Although it was located at the site of the former Baiyun Airport, which means that there were almost no residents within a radius of one kilometer, it delivered far better than expected performance after it was opened. It attracted an average daily passenger flow of more than 70,000 in the first year of its opening, and the hotel and cinema inside the plaza were among the best performers among Wanda's own hotels and cinemas nationwide. Many local people were just curious about how we could make it happen. When one of the group's independent shareholders attended a gathering for entrepreneurs in Guangzhou and sailed along the Pearl River after supper, he was asked whether Wanda implements a group-wide military-like management style and whether it is true that mistakes are punished with the whip, and that this is the reason why employees are able to pull off a project so quickly. He replied that it is Wanda's culture of execution that makes it happen. In other words, nothing is impossible. Military-like management and whip punishments would only drive employees away because it is difficult to build employee loyalty amid the fierce competition for talent.

Han Street, situated in Wuhan Central Culture District, represents something of a miracle because we had it completed and opened in just ten months. We completed the project so quickly because Wuhan was the main venue for the 2011 celebration of the 100th anniversary of the Xinhai Revolution, which brought an end to the reign of the Chinese emperors. Local officials hoped that we could complete it ahead of schedule because it was a landmark project for the special event. I agreed because I believed this was a golden opportunity to promote Wanda's image both at home and abroad. There were so many stories behind it. We took many measures to ensure that the project could be completed in time. It turned out that Han Street was very successful and really impressed officials at both city and provincial levels. As a new landmark in Wuhan, Han Street has a unique architectural style of the Republic of China period, boasting blended European and modern styles. Shortly after it was opened, a distinguished foreign guest visited Han Street in the company of Wuhan's Party chief and mayor. He later expressed his gratitude to the Wuhan government for preserving the traditional architecture of the Republic of China period so well. This is an illustration of the success of the project because the guest had failed to notice that the street was just newly opened.

Another project I'd like to talk about is the Changbai Mountain International Resort. It has a gross floor area of 1.2 million square meters and includes nine hotels, the largest ski resort in Asia, three golf courses and a small tourist town. The resort was completed and opened for business in just 26 months, another groundbreaking record registered by Wanda. In fact, we had to complete the project by August 2012 to ensure its successful bid for the right to host the winter events at the 2012 Asian Games. There were only six months available for construction on the Changbai Mountain due to its harsh weather. The mountain is under a one-meter layer of snow from October onwards, so we had no choice but to continue with the project's construction in winter to rush the construction work. I was deeply moved by our employees in overcoming tremendous difficulties. After the project was completed, as a special gesture, we held an award ceremony at the construction site where our construction teams and contractors of the project received rewards from hundreds of core managers from the Group who'd been flown in by plane. The resort reported strong performance shortly after it was opened with its first-year skier count standing at 50% higher than that of Yabuli Ski Resort, which has been open for more than 20 years. Furthermore, during this year's second ski season, the number of skiers grew by nearly 100% compared with the same period the year before. When the peak season occurs, the nine hotels in the resort with more than 5,000 beds are fully occupied, and it is extremely hard to get a room.

The next example is property sales. The construction of Qingdao Oriental Movie Metropolis was originally due to start in July 2013 with a sales target of three billion yuan for the first year it was open. However, due to land-related issues, there were only 16 days left from the day we obtained the pre-sale certificate for official sales until the end of the year. That is to say, we had to achieve the sales target, originally to be achieved in half a year, in just 16 days. The general manager of Wanda Qingdao Project Company said we would try and see after being asked by group leaders whether the sales target needed to be lowered. The general manager of Wanda Jiangxi heard about this, and he told the Qingdao general manager on the telephone that it would be too unrealistic to achieve the sales target in just 16 days unless there was a miracle. However, we were able to beat the target thanks to the efforts of our Qingdao Project Team and an effective marketing campaign. This is a striking characteristic of Wanda's culture of execution. We never say we can't do something, no matter what difficulties there may be. Acknowledging we can't do it in the first place is not a part of our corporate culture.

3. Clear system of rewards and penalties

Implementing a clear system of rewards and penalties serves as an important part of corporate management, but that is easier said than done. Such a system can't be implemented without strong execution. First, we are never stingy in offering awards. Take Wanda Wuhan Project Company, for example. The company, with a team comprising less than 100 members, beat its sales target of seven billion yuan in 2012 by recording unprecedented sales of more than 10 billion yuan through tremendously hard work. The salary of the team members at the Wuhan Project Company for the year would be several times higher than that of those at other Wanda Project Companies if bonus was paid based on their sales performance. In fact, we not only paid out bonuses to them in accordance with the Group's Target Responsibility Document, but also invited them to deliver speeches as role models during our Annual Outing. We offered them a platform for both fame and wealth. At Wanda, the salary gap can be tremendous even for the same position due to different execution outcomes, and nobody objects to this. Second, we dare to use punishment. A Vice President who used to be in charge of tendering and bidding at Wanda was fired by the Group for his interference in the tendering and bidding process for a cable project. He violated the Group's rules on the process by selecting a small company to be the successful bidder. The General Manager and Deputy General Manager of our Cost Department refused to sign off on the VP's selection in spite of enormous pressure from him. We launched an internal investigation against this VP after the General Manager of the Cost Department reported the matter to me and had this VP dismissed after verification. At Wanda, corporate rules are like high voltage lines, and those who touch them will get punished.

III. Management Model

A well-established management model is essential for successful execution. Our management model has three characteristics:

1. Centralized Authority at HQ

As China's society is in transition, corruption has become a serious problem, particularly in construction and real estate. In order to prevent corruption, we adopt a management model that features highly centralized authority at headquarters level as part of our effort to downplay the personal authority of the General Managers at our local project companies. The General Managers and Deputy General Managers of our project companies nationwide are subject to regular rotation depending on the job requirements. We have a rule that if any General Manager or Deputy General Manger refuses to comply with the company's arrangements, he or she will be dismissed. It is unlikely that Wanda will maintain positive growth momentum if our employees prefer to work only in major cities like Beijing and Shanghai. Of course, Wanda is not a company bereft of emotions, and it does consider the real difficulties of an employee's family. This has been the norm for quite some time, and cases of non-compliance have been rare.

2. Vertical Management

At headquarters, Wanda vertically manages its cost, finance, quality and safety systems so as to be able to control the key departments. Local companies are not allowed to meddle in personnel, finance or material matters of the vertical system, as these areas are managed by headquarters. Within the vertical system, personnel at the local companies are rotated after a three-year stint in order to avoid the formation of interest groups over time. A mechanism has been built so that top management within vertical systems and local companies can support and, at the same time, counterbalance each other.

3. Strengthened Supervision

Human nature is weak, and somebody's character is subject to change. I have often stated that we must rely on a system, not on loyalty. Loyalty is unreliable. The loyalty of this year may be gone next year. People may be incorruptible in the face of money, but still succumb to a beautiful woman. Therefore, Wanda's corporate management is based on strict rules. Our rules are developed with two features: first, we don't have confidence in anyone. It is from this starting point that we develop our rules. Second, in designing the system, we try to cover as many situations as we can, so as to minimize the number of loopholes and thus the chance of employees making mistakes. Take our bidding and tendering system, for example. We have built a "brand database" for all industry sectors that are relevant to our business. We have a special database for brands of electric cables, of elevators, and even of something as small as switches. Any company that is entered in the database must be a leader in its industry. Only the companies in the database can take part in the Wanda bidding and tendering process. The Wanda malls are so hot at the moment that spare retail space is in short supply. To prevent corruption in the bidding process, we have built a retailer database. We classify retailers into four tiers of A, B, C and D and Wanda Plazas into three grades of A, B and C. We have set a clear rule about which grade of Wanda Plazas bring in which tier of retailers. For example, the grade-A Wanda Plazas are only allowed to select tier-A and tier-B retailers, the grade-B Wanda Plazas may select tier-A, tier-B and tier-C retailers and the grade-C Wanda Plazas are only allowed to select tier-D retailers. The purpose of this rule is to minimize personal involvement in our bidding and tendering process. Many have asked me whether this rule has a negative effect on the development of individual capabilities and thus on the growth of the enterprise. But if we look at the situation on the ground, the reverse is true: not only has this rule had no negative impact on company growth, it has actually hastened it.

We have also built a strong audit team. Personally, I do not take charge of specific business lines, but I am the Head of the Audit Department, which is the equivalent of the Party's disciplinary commission and the Wanda "watch dog." The team is known for its strong expertise and has established Group-wide authority. It offers a strong deterrent to irregular practices within the Group. After completing audit work at the local companies nationwide, the Audit Department will issue – depending on audit results – a Management Letter, Notice of Rectification or Audit Notification Letter. If a Management Letter is issued, it means no punishment will be incurred; if a Notice of Rectification is issued, the Department will put forward areas of improvements and punishments may follow; if Audit Notification Letter is issued, the most severe consequences will occur with someone being dismissed or subject to a heavier punishment.

IV. Relying on technology to drive execution

It is important that we rely on information technology (IT) to drive execution at Wanda.

1. High degree of IT

We built an Information Centre and recruited a lot of overseas talent ten years ago when most companies had little awareness of the role of IT. The top management at the center is equivalent to vice-president level, the same as other business lines like Hotel and Commercial Management within the Group. Several years ago, we achieved office automation, moving from personal computers to mobile terminals. The mobile terminals were developed in-house and have greatly enhanced our efficiency as they can be accessed even on business trips. At Wanda, all our projects are required to be managed using an information-based approach. For example, cameras have been installed at all project sites, and mobile recording will be used to cover blind spots and uploaded to our information system so that the progress of each project can be monitored at HQ. The tendering and bidding process for our projects is conducted online too. Due to our enormous amount of investment in building advanced information systems, we were named one of the world's top 100 information-based companies, the only private company from China, by a globally recognized information magazine.

2. Modular Planning

We place particular emphasis on planning. We have established a Planning Department and put in place a wide range of start-of-construction plans, cost plans, profit plans, cash flow plans, revenue plans, recruitment plans, etc. Each plan is broken down into annual plans, monthly plans and weekly plans. Our plan-making process lasts three months – from September to December – and I will sign off all the plans by December 5. In other words, by the end of November, the General Manager of each business line of the Group will have a clear idea of the amount of money that should be earned and spent and how many employees should be hired for the next year.

Given the complexity of commercial property development, we have developed a modular planning software program through years of R&D efforts. The development cycle of a Wanda Plaza is typically around two years. We divide the entire cycle from construction to opening into nearly 400 specific plans, such as when to get project drawings done, the project status at a specific time, when to start the tenant acquisition process and when tenants can start decorating their stores inside the plaza. These specific plans are classified into three different levels, based on their degree of importance. The most important plans are managed by the President, less important ones by the Vice President and the least important ones by the Project Company. All these plans will be recorded in our information system. A green light on the system means that a given plan is completed successfully, and a yellow light means that a given plan is not completed as scheduled. If the yellow light is on for a whole week, it will turn into a red light and the responsible person will be punished. In order not to cause multiple delays in a year, we also stipulate that three yellow lights add up to a red light and punishments vary for failing to complete specific plans at different levels. If a yellow light is on, the Vice President in charge must come up with ideas to catch up on delayed projects, and he will be replaced if he fails to generate effective solutions to solve the problem in two months. That is why no project at Wanda is delayed for a few months or even half a year and can't eventually be opened. We have built a talent pool and established relevant regulations as to how many talented individuals need to be recruited for a company within the Group and what percentage of candidates should be placed in the pool. We never hesitate to spend more on talent-pool development at the Group. Take the position of General Manager at Project Companies for example. If there are 100 incumbent General Managers at the Project Company level, five General Managers will stand by at the HQ level. The replacement of any General Manager can occur at any time. The modular planning software platform is a critical tool to ensure that all projects can be opened for business on time. There is a famous saying at Wanda, "If you get stuck, look at your computer for help." All you need to do is to focus on the specific plans that you are responsible for. Our software program has received worldwide patents, and we have applied for patent protection in the EU and the U.S..

3. Huiyun Intelligent Management System

The Huiyun Intelligent Management System is an exclusive system developed by Wanda. The management and monitoring of shopping malls used to be done by isolated systems. For example, the electro-mechanical system, fire control system and energy conservation system have their respective functions, and such an isolated and disconnected mode of management and monitoring not only leads to a waste of human resources but also makes it difficult to prevent human errors. We have learnt painful lessons from it in the past. This is why we are prompted to find ways to prevent any incidents. We successfully developed the Huiyun system in 2013 after years of R&D. I named it Huiyun, which means Smart Cloud. The system is designed to centralize all fire control, water heating, air conditioning, energy conservation and safety monitoring systems installed in Wanda Plazas and hotels to ensure that all information is displayed on a single ultra-large screen. Our goal is to build a smart monitoring system across the board. For example, when a staff member is about to change his or her shift, the system will automatically send a message to the staff member on the next shift as a kind reminder. And if the system detects few people in a certain area, it will automatically reduce air conditioning volume to save energy. This system has been used in four Wanda Plazas on a pilot basis and is set to be deployed in all Wanda Plazas and hotels nationwide.

Our execution, which I believe is the strongest in China, if not globally, stems from a comprehensive list of factors, such as our established systems, corporate culture and technological innovation. Execution is one of our secrets of success. We reported 380 billion yuan of assets and nearly190 billion yuan of revenue last year and assets and revenue this year will exceed 450 billion and 250 billion, respectively. Assuming that our annual growth slows down to 15% sequentially beyond 2015, our assets, annual revenue and profit will still reach more than one trillion yuan, US$100 billion and US$10 billion by 2020, respectively, putting us on track to be one of the world's top 100 companies. Moreover, we are striving to become a multinational company with at least 20%-30% of our revenue coming from overseas operations by then. Our ambition is based on our efforts to prove that Chinese private companies are able to become internationally recognized players by competing with other players in the market and to win honor for Chinese companies, particularly Chinese private companies. Execution is our vital key to being a world leading company. The *History of the Former Han • Biography of Jia Yi* teaches us that the body controls the arms and the arms control the fingers, a metaphor that means handling a task will be simple and direct with the appropriate tools.

Thank you very much.

Q&A

Q: I am with a multinational company. I wonder whether your military background had anything to do with Wanda's corporate culture.

Wang Jianlin: Is there a direct relationship between a military background and success? The answer is "yes." I am not saying that everyone with a military background can make it big. But many successful entrepreneurs used to serve in the military, e.g. Liu Chuanzhi, Wang Shi, Ren Zhengfei and I. A survey conducted by the world-renowned Forbes magazine in 2003 found that more than 30% of 5,000 Chairpersons, CEOs and Presidents from the world's top 500 companies graduated from West Point. Of course, West Point students are elites themselves because the academy is known for its stringent selection procedure with a 40% elimination rate. The most important thing for West Point students to learn is to develop a strong will and set a firm goal, which lays a solid foundation for success.

The two most important factors for success are innovation and persistence. Never stop pursuing innovation, and never give in to setbacks. Otherwise success will be impossible. My military background has something to do with our corporate culture, but there is no absolute relationship between them. Therefore, a military background does not necessarily guarantee success.

Q: I am an MBA 2013 student at China Europe International Business School (CEIBS). How does Wanda instil its culture of execution across senior management at the Company?

Wang Jianlin: I am invited to talk about execution here today because it seems to you that I am successful. One of the most defining characteristics of my success is that I've never had full trust in books, so-called masters and foreign ideas.

A successful entrepreneur must bear in mind that you cannot simply copy models that have been proved by successful entrepreneurs. Qi Baishi, a well-known Chinese painter, and there's a famous saying of his: 'those who learn my painting style may make progress, while those devoted to imitating have no future at all.' Please don't take what I talk about here today as teaching material.

Wanda's proven model may be suitable for companies in the same industry and size bracket of around 100 billion yuan, but small and medium-sized enterprises (SMEs) and start-ups are quite different from Wanda and the industries where they operate are also different. Therefore, these SMEs and start-ups must explore and find models that are the most appropriate to them. This is why I always say that you should not trust those books talking about success, like "100 ways to be successful," or "30 approaches to beat your competitors." They are all nonsense. What I talk about today is just for your information.

We are going to add around 20,000 new employees this year to take our workforce from 103,000 to 120,000. With so many new employees on board, we launched the Wanda Academy in Langfang, Hebei Province, with an investment of nearly 800 million yuan, to instil our corporate culture among them and to help them gain a clear understanding of our business. The Wanda Academy can seat more than 3,000 people and offers no diploma-based education but mainly short-term training.

What disappoints me is that we can't find the right people from universities, where high-quality personnel in services, retail, e-commerce and business management are scarce. So other companies are trying to lure our employees away. We have no other choice but to strengthen our training programs, which have achieved a better-than-expected outcome. We have just completed the task of developing teaching materials used by the academy and have published two books named *Commercial Property Investment and Development* and *Commercial Property Operating Management*. We will also publish our thoughts and ideas over time with an intention to help you avoid setbacks.

Q: I am with a mobile Internet company. I believe that Wanda's shareholding structure is conducive to maintaining the Group's strong execution. Do you have any suggestions for start-ups?

Wang Jianlin: Shareholding structures and modern enterprise systems are not the same thing. It is difficult to say and conclude which one is better, a company with a major shareholding structure or one with a professional management system. Major shareholders may be concerned more about the companies they own. For example, AMC Entertainment reversed its long years of losses the first year when we became its major shareholder. I am not a savior, of course. AMC used to have five shareholders with almost the same shareholding, and none of them really cared about the company. I told AMC management when we first met that we would sign a five-year contract and they would be offered 10% of the profit as their dividends. After these shareholders were devoted to the management of the company, it reported profit in the first year of the contract and earned more in the second year. This is just the pro side of having a major shareholder at a company. Of course, we cannot overlook the fact that there are still major shareholders who lead their companies into collapse. By contrast, professional managers are not willing to care about the long-term interests of the companies they help run and will never pursue investments that deliver returns after a five-to-eight-year horizon.

Success can be achieved whether it is a company with a professional management system or a major shareholding structure. Family-run businesses have the longest history of any business type in the world, and there are many family businesses in Europe. That is to say that an appropriate model can be a family-run company, a company controlled by a major shareholder or one run by a professional manager. Just like an advertising slogan said, "Only your feet know how comfortable your shoes are."

Q: I am with China Telecom. You plan to generate 30% of Wanda's total revenue from overseas markets. Lenovo and Huawei are just two good examples of Chinese companies seeking to go global. How do you view the "Going Global" strategy from a strategic perspective?

Wang Jianlin: Our target is to generate 20%-30% of our future revenue from overseas. It is an inevitable choice for a company to pursue multinational operations when it achieves a considerable scale. We have set a target to achieve more than US$100 billion of revenue in five or six years. If we continue to focus our business on mainland China, it will be somewhat difficult for us to accomplish this target because China's economic growth is slowing overall.

Our pursuit of the "Going Global" strategy is based on the following reasons from a strategic perspective:

First, to achieve our long-term target. Our current vision is "International Wanda, Centennial Business." However, when the company was established, its vision was to "Be Honest and Smart." This helped us to navigate our initial difficulties and served as a reminder for us not to be fooled by other companies. When we made some profit around 1998, we upgraded our corporate culture and changed our vision to "Creating Common Prosperity through Serving the Community," and as we grew, we further changed it to "International Wanda, Centennial Business." International is an implication of our aim to become an international company and centennial business stands for the company's pursuit of long-term and sustainable growth. To do this, we must go global.

Second, the need to diversify risks. Internationalization can help to do this. It is important for private companies, in particular, to go global.

Third: to increase revenue. A company can only grow faster and larger through internationalization and mergers and acquisitions. If you look at the world's top 500 companies, you will find that there is not a single company that has thrived through organic growth, and each company on the Fortune 500 list has completed at least an M&A deal before making it onto the list.

Q: I am with an air and chemical products company owned by a multinational company. Will Wanda's business model work in small cities and towns in China? Will policy and political risks in foreign countries hinder Wanda's vision to go global?

Wang Jianlin: Wanda's business model also works in small cities and towns, and we already have a few projects in some countries. We divide Wanda Plazas into three levels of A, B and C, and they will spread throughout many countries to expand the room for development.

Wanda's "Going Global" strategy does not necessarily mean that we will simply copy our property business model in overseas markets. We will not invest in shopping malls as we pursue our goal of being an international company because there is almost no room for development in light of the high degree of maturity of the business model overseas and strict regulations on the retail sector in the U.S., UK and EU. For example, there are regulations concerning the specific area of retail space and whether a land parcel can be redeveloped into a shopping mall. China should learn from these developed countries in terms of retail layout.

We plan to expand our culture and tourism businesses to foreign markets. M&A is the only growth option available to us if we do the real estate business overseas. It is based on a prerequisite that we are only interested in projects that are related to our businesses. Our "Going Global" effort does not mean we strive to become an international property company. Instead, it means we strive to become an international company in corporate strategy, culture and development. Now our "Going Global" effort focuses on building premium five-star hotels overseas. Like foreign companies who have opened hotels in China, we can also open hotels in overseas countries. Our goal is to build 10-20 premium five-star hotels around the world within the next decade. Of course, we won't rule out the possibility of acquiring a large-scale multinational hotel chain. It would be a good thing if Chinese travellers could stay in Chinese hotels abroad.

Q: Our company is a private company engaged in energy-saving and new energy vehicles. A company's internal execution will be affected by many external factors. For example, there are a number of constraints for project development, such as site selection, demolition, permit and fire safety inspection. How can you obtain government approvals and ensure that all projects can be opened on time?

Wang Jianlin: It is a very professional question. It is indeed the case that it is easy to perform internal control, while it is difficult to perform external control. This is particularly true in terms of permits. Many people have asked me over the years why Wanda is able to obtain permits without giving bribes. The secret is our innovative business model. There will not be an issue if your model is exclusive and sufficiently unique.

We started developing the Wanda Plaza project many years ago, when other companies had no clear idea about the real estate business, and it has become our signature brand following its evolution from first generation to second- and third-generation integrated urban complexes. We have now moved into the culture and tourism sectors, while seeking multinational development, and many companies are still hesitant to enter the real estate market.

Furthermore, the land plots we have acquired are cleared land and from our own experience, it is absolutely impossible to open any Wanda mall for business if a fire-safety permit is not obtained. At the moment, we have established a Business Design Institute, Culture & Tourism Design Institute and Hotel Design Institute. The reason why we have to establish our own design institutes is that we try to minimize design flaws by strictly following business and fire-safety standards. We have learned the varied standards in eastern, western and central China and do our best to meet relevant requirements so that we seldom face approval barriers. Of course, it is also a result of the hard work of our local teams.

Q: I am from Hangzhou, Zhejiang Province. Wanda was engaged in the residential property business before it moved into the commercial property sector. Did you hear any objections from people inside the company at that time? Was there any struggle about this decision?

Wang Jianlin: Wanda underwent its first transformation when it turned from a local company into a nationwide group. We are a pioneer of pursuing inter-regional development in China. We expanded to Guangzhou in 1993. However, when we applied to register a local company in the city, the local administration for industry and commerce refused to approve our application, saying that there were no relevant government regulations. They asked why a Dalian-based company applied to set up a company in Guangzhou. We had to reach out to a local real estate company and agree to spend two million yuan in renting the company's account and paying annual management fees into it so we could successfully set up a branch in the city. Our second transformation was completed after we shifted to commercial properties from residential properties, and our third transformation was from commercial properties to cultural tourism. The fourth transformation, under way in recent years, has been for us to accomplish our vision of

Going Global and turning Wanda from a domestic enterprise into a world-leading multinational enterprise.

There were different voices during our second transformation asking why we moved into the commercial property market when our residential property business was a great success. At the beginning, we had no idea about how to operate a commercial property business and were caught in 222 lawsuits as a defendant in the first three years. We would probably have given up if we had not been persistent enough at that time. Many of my subordinates asked if it was worth it. I told them that commercial properties could generate long-term stable cash flows while residential commercial couldn't. In fact, I had not realized the risk associated with the completion of China's urbanization process. It seems to me now that the risk has become greater as China's urbanization rate could reach 70%-75% in 15 years from 52% at the moment. This means that demand for residential properties will be greatly decreased. Although the residential property sector will not disappear, its business model featuring massive development, rapid turnover and enormous cash flows will cease to exist. Long-term, stable cash flows must be taken into account if a company wants to achieve long-term development. Every business owner should bear in mind "long-term" and "stable," which serve as the keys to running a successful business.

There were also struggles as we expanded into the commercial property sector. In this case, the benefit of having a major shareholder made itself felt. I told my team that we would keep going till the five-year mark and if we saw no turnaround, then we would just exit the market. It seemed that we began to have some idea about this business in 2004, when the construction of the Shanghai Wujiaochang Plaza, Ningbo Yinzhou Plaza and Beijing CBD Plaza started at the same time. I said if these three projects proved to be successful, we would keep going with the business. The success of these projects helped us strengthen our confidence to move forward, until today. So perseverance is extremely important for innovation and start-ups.

Chapter Four

Innovation

Our Unique Competitive Edge

25 April, 2012 – A speech at Tsinghua University

At the request of Tsinghua University, Wang Jianlin delivered a speech entitled "Innovation and Competitiveness Illustrated with Wanda as An Example" during the Entrepreneurs' Lectures held at the Tsinghua University School of Economics and Management on 25 April, 2012. In the speech, Wang encouraged the students to think outside the box, to have the courage to do things nobody had ever attempted to do, and to dare think of things nobody had ever thought of.

I. Development history of Wanda

Founded in 1988, Wanda started as a small company with a registered capital of 500,000 yuan. After 24 years of dedicated development, it has now established itself as the leader of private enterprises in China, ranking among the largest Chinese companies across the four core indicators, i.e. assets, revenue, profit and tax contribution. Wanda created 89,600 new jobs last year, accounting for 0.8% of the national total. In particular, the company recruited 20,000 university graduates, making it the largest graduate recruiter and job creator in China. Over the past 24 years, Wanda donated an aggregate of 2.8 billion yuan in cash – 260 million in 2011 alone, ranking it as the largest corporate donor of all Chinese enterprises in aggregate terms and in terms of annual donation.

As for the reasons for the company's rapid development: firstly, Wanda owes its success to the macroeconomic platform created by the state. The Chinese economy growing at an annual rate of 9.5% provided the company with an enormous space for development. Secondly, the rise of Wanda as a leading private company has been driven ultimately by innovation. The development history of Wanda is a process of continuous innovation. My pet phrase these years has been, "a degree from Tsinghua or Peking University can't beat having guts." An old Chinese saying goes "seek wealth in danger," meaning that if you risk nothing, you gain nothing. Apart from talent and hard work, the key to success lies in being bold – daring to do things and daring to try things. This is different from using brute force – an enterprising person puts in hard work following a well-targeted plan and won't be daunted by setbacks, while brute force equates to blind actions based on mere wishful thinking and without prior planning. Wanda achieved rapid growth through these years, and the reason is its development has been driven by an "innovative spirit."

II. Innovation at Wanda

Over the past 24 years, Wanda has implemented the innovation strategy in six "phases."

1. Urban redevelopment

Wanda used to be a very small firm when it was founded in 1988. Back then, "planned quotas" were required for all real estate projects. Property developers had to obtain quotas before applying for land acquisition. The quotas were all allocated by the National Planning Commission, and only the three state-owned developers in Dalian were allocated quotas. Wanda was not one of them, so we had to buy quotas from them. It was like "seeking survival in the cracks." I went to the Dalian government and told them that we would accept any project as long as the profit was enough to sustain ourselves, regardless of location. At that time, there was a shantytown on the Beijing Street to the north of the municipal government. It was viewed as the shame of the entire city. The government asked the three state-owned property developers to redevelop the area, but none were willing to take it. Having heard what I asked for, the government offered to approve planning quotas if I accepted the shantytown project.

We estimated that the cost of development of the shantytown project on Beijing Street was 1,200 yuan per square meter, but back then the most expensive apartments in Dalian were priced at 1,100 yuan a meter. To make the project profitable, we had to find a way of selling the apartments at 1,500 yuan per square meter. We made a number of innovations:

1. We decided to fit all apartments with aluminum windows, which were very rare in Northeast China in those days.

2. All apartments came with security doors, which had barely become mainstream in the local housing market.

3. In those days, virtually no living rooms had windows, and we made it a standard in our design.

4. Bathrooms used to be a luxury enjoyed only by cadres at the county level or above, but every apartment in the Beijing Street project came with a separate bathroom. We innovated our marketing approach with a bold decision – that is, investing 80,000 yuan in a Hong Kong or Taiwanese TV drama. TV series from Hong Kong and Taiwan were very popular at the time, and our sponsorship made the Beijing Street Project a household name in Dalian. The innovations produced dramatic results. All the 1,000 or more apartments in the project were sold out within one month at a record average price of 1,600 yuan per square meter. The company made nearly 10 million yuan in profit. This is when we made the first "pot of gold." More importantly, Wanda was the first company in China with experience in urban redevelopment, offering a new approach to our corporate development. Ever since then, we knew that this approach worked and never looked back.

We took on urban redevelopment projects at different locations, and the company scaled up in a few years. By 1992, Wanda posted sales revenue of around two billion yuan, accounting for 25% of the real estate market in Dalian.

2. Nationwide development

In early 1992, Deng Xiaoping made an important speech during his tour of southern China. He called for bolder reforms at a faster pace. It made my blood boil with excitement. At that time they said, "Guangdong is the best place to make money," so we decided to venture into the real estate market in Guangdong. It was against the government's rules to register companies outside one's province of residence, but where there is a will, there is a way. We had a local company, SOCT Real Estate (Shenzhen Overseas Chinese Town), register a branch company for us, and we paid them service fees. We developed a 400,000 square-meter housing project in Guangzhou. Even though the project didn't bring us substantial profit due to our limited understanding of the local culture and limited cost control and management capabilities, we gained confidence, and Wanda became the first property developer in China to pioneer cross-regional project development.

With increased confidence and hardened resolve, Wanda became unstoppable and started full-scale cross-regional development from 1997 onward. To date, we have invested in more than 80 Chinese cities in the 23 provinces, excluding Guizhou and Qinghai, in all four directly administered municipalities and in the five autonomous regions excluding Xinjiang and Tibet, making us a leading real estate developer with the largest cross-regional business presence in the country.

3. Business model innovation

Wanda has adopted the following strategies in terms of business model innovation:

1. "Gold digging"

I realized in early 2000 that housing property development entails inherent risks. First, no housing property developer can last 100 years. As the urbanization process comes to an end, the demand for housing properties declines, and most developers will disappear. This is decided by the nature of the industry. Second, the cash flow in housing property development is inherently unstable – cash flow is healthy only when there are developed properties for sale, but it disappears once the properties are sold out and the next property design and development cycle begins. Third, I was struck by the tragedies that befell two of our employees. One of them was diagnosed with cancer and the other with liver disease. Social insurance was non-existent at that time, and private companies had to bear the costs themselves. I did what was believed to be impossible. The company paid for medical treatment for the two employees. It cost the company over three million yuan in total. I couldn't help thinking that Wanda was still young – in its teenage years. What would we do when we have tens of thousands of employees 20 or 30 years later? Many of them would be old, retired, and need medical-expense coverage. For the sake of my colleagues as well as myself, I proposed two central requirements for corporate development – that is, we needed to ensure lasting and stable cash flow. How could we achieve this? We decided to switch to commercial properties after thorough deliberation and discussions. We are all experts in property construction, and can recruit professionals in the field of tenant attraction, of which we had limited knowledge. The meeting lasted three days…we call it the "Zunyi Conference" (the most decisive meeting in the history of the Chinese Communist Party, and we laid down the correct development direction for the company.

After we made the decision to switch to commercial property, the first thing that came to my mind was "gold digging." Before that, Wanda developed a number of rental properties – seven to eight small shopping malls and restaurants, but severe rent arrears forced us to set up a collection team. To get around this problem, we decided to only cooperate with big companies for rental properties, Fortune 500 companies, and we started with Wal-Mart. I tried to make an appointment with Wal-Mart's vice president in charge of business development, and finally met him several months later, after countless rejections. He laughed at me after hearing my proposition, as if saying: how would such a small company dare to propose cooperation with Wal-Mart? I told him repeatedly that we could offer favorable terms, and he eventually agreed to try it out with a small project first, without negotiating about cooperation. After that, I went to Shenzhen in person to sell my proposal to Wal-Mart's CEO in the Asia Pacific. After dozens of visits in the following six months or so, Wal-Mart finally agreed to cooperate with us on the first Wanda Plaza in Changchun. We used every means at our disposal to make the project a success, to ensure that the retail giant would be convinced to continue cooperation with us. Our hard work paid off, and Wal-Mart agreed to sign a strategic cooperation agreement with us when we opened the fifth Wanda Plaza. With such an agreement in hand, we persuaded more multinationals to collaborate with us, including Chinese brands such as Suning and Guomei. They played a significant role in the development of Wanda Plaza during the early years. Standing on the shoulders of giants, we could see further and develop faster. The strategy was successful!

We benefited from cooperating with large multinationals not only in terms of business development, but it also provided us with inspiration for corporate management and culture. Today, Wanda has the largest number of retailer partners among all commercial property developers in China. We have signed strategic cooperation agreements with over 5,000 companies, of which nearly 300 are multinationals. And the relationships between the retailers and us have been completely reversed. Wanda now sets the rules, and the retailers follow. As they say in business, "A shop can dictate to its customers if it's strong enough, and vice versa." This story proves that, in addition to courage, a necessary quality for successful entrepreneurs is perseverance, without fear of rejection.

2. Industry chain

A problem came after the first several Wanda Plazas. That is, no Chinese design institutes were capable of producing satisfactory designs for such projects – most of them specialized in designing housing properties or department stores, not shopping centers. We had to hire companies from Australia and the U.S. The drawbacks of this include high design costs and a long design period, making it impossible to catch up with the development of the company.

It dawned on me that if we take commercial property as our lifelong career and the core value of the company, we must have our own design team and management company. We can't put our fate in the hands of others. Therefore, from 2003 onward, Wanda set up its own design institute and business management company. Our design institute is the only one in China specializing in commercial property planning and design, focusing on the design of shopping centers and five-star hotels. Consisting of more than 200 staff members, the institute is capable of independently designing shopping centers and five-star hotels, including architecture, structure, decoration and electromechanical engineering. As well as minimizing design costs, it makes Wanda the owner of relevant intellectual properties, giving it core competitiveness. In business management theory, it is believed that third-rate companies sell products, second-rate companies sell brands, and first-rate companies sell standards. Wanda commercial property design institute developed the Chinese shopping mall fire code, evaluation criteria, management standards, etc. for the Ministry of Public Security, Ministry of Housing and Urban-Rural Development and the Ministry of Commerce, attesting to our status as the pacesetter in the commercial property industry.

Since its founding, the Wanda commercial property management company has played a significant supporting role in the development of Wanda Plazas. Up until 2011, the company maintained a super-high rent collection rate of above 99.6% for six consecutive years, ranking Wanda as the best real estate company worldwide in rent collection terms.

3. Standardization

Having established a suitable business model and a fully developed industry chain, Wanda focused its efforts on standardization, as rapid development can only be achieved through standardized operations.

The first task was to establish a brand pool. All of Wanda's partner retailers and products were divided into different categories and included in the pool. It is a rule at Wanda that only brands included in the pool are eligible for cooperation with us. The brands were divided into A, B, C and D categories, and Wanda Plazas were divided into A, B and C classes. A-class stores can only cooperate with retailers in category A or B; B-class stores can only cooperate with retailers in category A, B or C; and only C-class stores can cooperate with all brands across the four categories. The brand pool is reviewed and adjusted once a year, with brands reported with major incidents blacklisted on a real-time basis, such that the retailers are accurately assessed to effectively prevent internal corruption.

Secondly, we adopt modular project management where the entire commercial property development process is divided into nearly 400 segments in a chronological sequence with strict regulations as to the specific tasks to be performed by relevant departments in each segment. The segments are further divided into three tiers, corresponding to different management levels. For example, presidents are only responsible for tier-1 segments, vice presidents for tier-2 segments, and project companies for tier-3 segments. Modular management software is then developed based on the regulations so that in November of each year, specific day-to-day tasks planned for every individual unit and employee for the following year can be entered into the system. Performance appraisal is automatically carried out by the information system. If a given employee fails to complete the scheduled progress by the preset deadline, the "yellow light" turns on by way of warning; if s/he fails to catch up within the time limit, the "red light" goes on. Once it happens, related managers will be penalized, and the penalties are connected with their income. This way, all management activities at Wanda become fully standardized as modular process management.

4. Culture industry

Wanda Plazas are not limited to shopping and also include catering, entertainment, etc. They are designed as "lifestyle centers" catering to a diverse range of consumer needs. In a bid to stimulate business growth, cultural businesses, such as cinema and buffet-style KTV (Karaoke Television), have been introduced to Wanda Plazas. We have been planning to increase the weight of cultural businesses in recent years, and have so far introduced a Central Cultural District, large-scale theatrical performance, filmmaking and screening, cultural and entertainment chains and Chinese calligraphy and painting collections.

1. Cinema

Wanda entered the film market because it had no other choice. At first, we didn't want to operate cinemas ourselves. Instead, our strategy was to live on property rent as the landlord. At first, we chose SMG (Shanghai Media Group) as our partner and signed an agreement with them. The idea was that they could grow with us. Unexpectedly, as we completed building the six cinemas half a year later, SMG replaced its manager, and the new manager decided not to go to any markets outside Shanghai. According to the agreement, we could have kept their 20 million yuan deposit as damages, but they insisted that if we withheld the deposit, it would cause a loss of state-owned assets, so we returned it. Besides, Wanda was not interested in earning this kind of money. We then talked to Time Warner, the largest cultural business group in the world and signed a close strategic cooperation agreement with it. Warner was very enthusiastic about the cooperation. However, China joined the WTO less than a year later, and the government banned foreign companies from entering cinema operations or acquiring more than 49% in any film company, meaning that Time Warner could no longer partner with us. We already had several cinemas in operation back then, and the question was whether we should take them over. I said during a board meeting that operating cinemas couldn't be any more difficult than developing two nuclear bombs and one satellite. As a result, Wanda set up its own cinema. To our surprise, Wanda cinemas that were losing money throughout the three years when they were managed by other companies, turned profitable in the first year of operation after the takeover. The cinemas have now become leaders in the industry. As of the end of this year, Wanda has opened 115 5-star cinemas equipped with 1,000 screens, making it the largest cinema chain in Asia.

2. Central cultural district

Wanda invested 50 billion yuan in constructing the Central Cultural District in Wuhan. This comprises 10 cultural projects featuring a film technology park and the "Han Show." (Han was the second imperial dynasty of China, contemporary with the Romans.) Opened in 2014, the film park brings together the latest film technologies and interactive entertainment in the world, and consists of a 4-D cinema, a 5-D cinema and flight, interaction, aerospace and disaster themeed cinemas, making it truly one-of-a-kind, and it was developed entirely by Wanda itself. We invested 2.5 billion yuan in the world-class "Han Show." The Central Cultural District in Wuhan is home to the largest library, Madame Tussauds, China's largest cinema city, buffet-style karaoke, five celebrity squares, a piano store and a Han-style theatre.

Wuhan Central Cultural District Phase I was opened in September 2011, and has been receiving over 100,000 visitors every day, ranking among the top 10 tourist attractions in Wuhan. Visitors to the Central Cultural District during the seven-day national holiday in 2011 totaled 2.45 million. As the only new tourist site reported by the National Holiday Office, it is hailed as a brand new cultural and leisure business model in urban areas.

3. Large-scale performance facilities

With an investment of 10 billion yuan, Wanda partnered with two heavyweight international artists to create five world-class events in China. One of them is Franco Dragone, one of the most celebrated theatre directors in the world, creator of the famous Las Vegas "O Show" and "Le Rêve – The Dream" and "The House of Dancing Water" in Macao, China; the other is Mark Fisher, one of the world's top architects, artistic director for the opening and closing ceremonies of the Beijing Olympics, Guangzhou Asian Games and the London Olympic Games.

4. A cultural entertainment chain

Wanda's Super Star KTV had 63 stores at the end of 2012, and rose to the No. 1 ranking in the karaoke business within just three years.

5. Traditional Chinese calligraphy and painting collections

Wanda started collecting Chinese calligraphy and paintings 20 years ago. At first it was driven purely by my personal interest. I listed the 100 greatest modern and contemporary Chinese painters with the guidance of established art connoisseurs and started collecting their masterpieces. Today, Wanda has earned a status among collectors comparable to that in the commercial property business. Our collections include around 1,000 great masterpieces by 100 renowned Chinese painters and calligraphers, and the company has participated in numerous international cultural events representing China.

5. Resort tourism

As our commercial property business took off, we were invited by the Jilin Provincial Government to develop resort tourism properties in the Changbai Mountains. This was a totally new business for us. Construction of Changbai Mountain International Resort started with an investment of 20 billion yuan, and the resort is due to open in July this year. The success of the Changbaishan resort boosted our confidence in resort property development, and we invested in similar projects in. For example, Xishuangbanna, a project that involves a sizable investment of 15 billion yuan. In recognition of our impressive achievements in the resort tourism industry in recent years, the International Association of Amusement Parks and Attractions (IAAPA), the world's largest general trade association for the resort and amusement park industries, accepted Wanda as a premium member. The IAAPA only has six premium members, including household names such as Disney, Universal Studios and Ocean Park. Wanda is the only premium member in Asia.

In addition to commercial properties, culture and tourism have become a central pillar business for Wanda. Throughout the past three years, I've been personally involved in cultural and tourism businesses and seldom asked about commercial properties. Judging by the long-term trend, the government has set out the long-term strategy for the domestic consumer market. Consumption in China will double from 15.7 trillion yuan in 2010 to 31 trillion in 2015, which translates into a net increase of 15 trillion yuan in market volume; domestic consumption will reach 62 trillion yuan by 2020, a 45 trillion net increase in market volume. Therefore, China will overtake the U.S. as the largest consumer market in the world. Wanda's development strategy conforms to the government's long-term plan and the general trend. The company is well on track to becoming a world-class player in the global cultural and resort markets in three to five years, and I believe that we'll contribute significantly to the Chinese economy as a whole. Real estate development is to make successful projects, commercial properties, but the cultural and tourism business is to make history. It's an achievement at a higher level.

6. Transnational development

Earlier this year, we developed a ten-year development strategy for Wanda. The main objective is to develop the company across borders. We coined the slogan that we don't want to be the "guys at the frontier." Our goal is to establish Wanda as a world-class multinational company in ten years. We'll announce a world-shaking cross-border acquisition this year. Besides this, Wanda will make direct investments overseas. We'll prove with concrete actions that Chinese private companies are also capable of growing into major multinational powers to dominate global competition.

III. Wanda's competitive advantages

Wanda boasts the following four competitive advantages.

1. Rapid development

Ever since its founding 24 years ago, Wanda has always maintained double-digit growth rates. During the past five years, it posted solid business development with year-on-year growth exceeding 35%. Our revenue is projected to hit 140 billion yuan by the end of 2012, and we are on our way to becoming a Fortune 500 company in this regard. By 2014, we expect Wanda Group's revenue to increase to 200 billion yuan, thereby ranking it among the Fortune 500 companies, with even better rankings in terms of net profit, valuation and assets. In other words, we'll be a world-class enterprise in three to five years.

2. The industry leader

Wanda is recognized as the leader in China and even the world in every business in which we operate. As of the end of this year, Wanda ranks number three in terms of property holding among all real estate companies worldwide; developing at the current rate, we'll be the largest real estate company in the world in 2015.

Wanda will become the owner of the world's largest five-star hotels at the end of the year, with 38 hotels in operation and another 40-odd projects under construction.

Wanda will become the largest cultural business operator in China by the end of the year; our cinemas are ranked No. 1 in Asia. The Wanda performance company will launch two projects in 2014, making it the global leader in the entertainment industry as well.

We are already recognized in the resort tourism industry as a leading global investor.

We have become one of the largest department store chains in China.

Of all the five businesses operated by Wanda, as the minimum target we aim to be the No. 1 market player in China. Our reference system is based on the global markets. There's nothing wrong with being No. 1 worldwide. All lawful, market-oriented and profitable enterprises should have the courage to be the top player. Wanda is the domestic and even global market leader in all of the five businesses. At the risk of sounding immodest, once Wanda has entered a market, whatever it is, no one else can be the leader there, not state-owned enterprises (SOEs) or even state-oriented enterprises. Given the fast growth of the private sector in China, the majority of Chinese companies will be privately owned in ten years.

3. Super strong profitability

The value of innovation lies in innovators' pricing power derived from the fact that they have something that others don't, which allows them to yield more profits than the competitors. For example, there are 130 cinema chains in China, and Wanda's screens account for less than 7% of the national total, but we generated 15% of the total revenue created by all Chinese cinemas combined. Each of our screens yields more than twice the average revenue and three times the average profit in the industry. These are the benefits that can be realized through innovative management.

4. Popularity

From Wanda Plazas to luxury hotels, and especially cultural and tourism businesses, the Wanda brand has been warmly received by local governments and local residents alike, wherever we've gone. We're one of the few enterprises managing to win the support of local governments as well as the people at the same time. A single Wanda Plaza creates almost 10,000 jobs and generates taxes of more than 100 million yuan, as well as stimulating regional economic growth. For these reasons, we have received invitations from many local governments vying to secure development projects with us, but we can only choose a third or even a quarter of them.

There are many factors contributing to success, such as environment, hard work, talent and so on, but the most crucial factor is being enterprising, having the courage to pioneer new things and new ideas, which is where success comes from. Only innovation can bring competitiveness, enabling a company to grow faster than its competitors.

Next, I'll answer your questions.

Q&A

Q: First, I'd like to ask…we've heard a lot about you and Wanda in the press recently, but you received the charity award at Zhongnanhai (central headquarters of the Chinese government). I think the award itself scotches speculation. What's your opinion on this? My second question is that as it's now unclear where the Chinese real estate market is heading, what's your opinion about the market trend as a veteran property developer? And what's your advice for Chinese home-buyers with urgent needs?

Wang Jianlin: To answer your first question, it's pretty natural to have speculation, and this is particularly true for well-known companies and well-known entrepreneurs. The Internet is very popular these days. People say whatever they want to say without any restrictions, especially about large groups like Wanda, given our explosive growth. There have been rumors recently that Wanda has connections with someone. My impression at first was that the rumors would disappear in a while, but they're still there, so Wanda made a solemn declaration. In fact, Wanda decided internally 15 years ago to abolish payments in cash altogether throughout the company, including our headquarters. No payments could be made in cash. The aim was to eliminate bribery at the source. We're one of the few private companies in China who can say, "we don't use bribery" with confidence. Most companies can't. The rumors have started to disappear lately. Whether or not Wanda will be implicated in anything ultimately depends on our business development. If I can still speak here next year, that means the company's doing well.

Besides, Wanda aimed to build an international enterprise that lasts 100 years in as early as 2002 when the company went through an upgrade of corporate culture. We are only 24 years old and have 76 years to go to 100. During the next 76 years, it won't always be easy and there will certainly be peaks and valleys. We've gone through six real estate market regulations in the past 24 years. For the first three regulations, it was called "rectification" and later changed to macro-level regulation. There'll be at least several more to come in the next ten years. The economy always goes through peaks and valleys. A company must be able to sustain itself through low times and maintain normal development, if it aspires to last 100 years. As for myself, if I couldn't take criticism and rumors, I wouldn't be successful in the first place.

For the second question, my opinion about the real estate industry, let me be straightforward, the Chinese real estate market will remain upbeat for the next 15 to 20 years at least. The urbanization rate in China currently stands only at 51%, and China's urbanization actually includes both cities and small towns; towns with a population of 3,000 or 5,000 people should not be counted as urban areas and therefore should be excluded when calculating the urbanization rate. Even if urbanization has reached 51% in China, 49% of Chinese people are still living in rural areas. The global urbanization rate is 60%, and that of relatively developed countries at the medium level or above is 75-80%. China may not be fully urbanized like the U.S. and European countries, but at least 70% of the Chinese population will live in urban areas in the future. It means that more than 300 million people will migrate to cities. Urbanization is the biggest driver for long-term economic growth in China. Besides, the industrialization process has not been completed in China, meaning that the real estate industry will remain on an upward trend from a long-term perspective during the next 15-20 years, in view of the ongoing urbanization process. It's just been suppressed by the regulation policies in the last couple of years, adding to the bubbles and risks that build up amid the recent explosive growth. However, from a long-term perspective, the real estate industry will continue to grow steadily and is still on an upward trajectory.

Q: Since Wanda has completed many sensational projects, how do you control the risks? Considering the number of good projects, how would you decide which projects to invest in and which to reject? Another question...many of your ideas are visionary for Chinese and by international standards as well, so how do you communicate with the government and convince them of your highly creative ideas?

Wang Jianlin: Risk control is the most important thing among other priorities for a company. This is particularly true for enterprises of a medium size or above. If a company doesn't understand risk control, it would be impossible for it to develop...develop quickly. Risk control, first and foremost involves risk management in decision making. When it comes to project selection at Wanda, the benefits of a project are weighed against the potential risks at an early stage. Our development department is responsible for selecting development projects and doing the planning, and the investment and cost-control departments engage each other in debates about the feasibility of the project. The analysis report can be drafted only after a consensus has been reached between them. Wanda has developed a template over the years. We have 50 questions (there used to be 100 questions, and we combined them into 50). We require that all the 50 questions must be answered in the report, and the answers must be substantiated with statistics. When a project (proposal) reaches the decision-making level...say they propose 50 projects, and we can only adopt 20, how do we choose? We rank the projects in terms of city size, project profitability, etc., and those with the best rankings are selected.

There are other types of risk control...financial risk control, for example. In many companies, there is only one accountant, one manager and one cashier. They can collude with each other and embezzle millions of yuan. Our information management system at Wanda includes a signature approval process where money can't be paid out until all people in the system have signed for and approved the payment. Wanda's financial and cost control systems adopt the vertical management model. The headquarters controls the finances of local branches in each system, without interference from any local companies, and personnel appointment, removal, bonuses and transfers are all controlled by the headquarters. To prevent collusion more effectively, both systems operate within the same business module, and every three years, position-transfers are carried out for all employees involved. There are a series of other measures in place to ensure effective risk management. Therefore, if a company performs well, it's not simply because it has achieved excellent business development. Risk control is a more important factor. Creating a big company alone won't make you successful. A successful entrepreneur should prioritize stability and sustainability.

Your second question is how to gain popularity. Firstly, we need to develop a good product model. We need to develop products that only we can make, not anyone else, or even if they can, they can't make it as well as we do. While doing business, we want the clients to come to us, rather than having our people ask for their help. Wanda created the commercial property model, and we're developing performance venues for our cultural business. We brought together the best artists in the world, Dragone and Fisher, and due to competition considerations, we signed exclusive agreements with them to tie them only to us, prohibiting them from cooperating with any other companies in the world in the next several years. Similarly, we secured close cooperation with the world's most renowned theme park and amusement park design firms. We promise to develop at least five large projects in China in the next 10-15 years, integrating all human resources, intellectual properties, etc. making it difficult for others to enter these businesses, even if they obtain enough funding. We make our products popular so that we no longer need to beg for help from others. If we beat all the competition in a competitive business, others will naturally come to us for help.

Q: I'm originally from Qiqihar in Heilongjiang Province. My question is what are your thoughts about real estate developers in tier-three or tier-four cities like Qiqihar? I'm always interested in hearing the latest news about you, and I found that you're not very keen to appear at public events or give speeches in front of large audiences. I hope you could lecture more in schools to inspire the students with your success story and your charisma and encourage them to start their own businesses. There are many ambitious and experienced students in Beijing. I'd like to extend an informal invitation to you on behalf of my teachers and classmates.

Wang Jianlin: My advice to all companies in tier-one, two, three or four cities alike is that if you want to survive in the housing property business, you must innovate. Our target for 2020 is to lower the proportion of real estate revenues to less than 50% of our total revenue. We have set the same target for profit structure. The state is calling for economic restructuring and adjusting the growth model. How can we meet the objectives? The national strategy can be fulfilled only if all companies restructure their businesses and adjust development models. If we stick to the old housing property development model, we'll have less and less room for growth. Above all, as the affordable housing program progresses, the market will get smaller and smaller.

As for public lectures, I'm not against speaking in public, but I've got a very tight schedule. I take fewer than five days off a year. Feng Lun once said that I was the busiest entrepreneur in China…(he even asked) if I wanted to earn all the money in the world. The truth is that I'm not interested in making money. I've already made it clear that I'd donate 90% of my properties to charity. I have been appointed honorary president of China Charity Federation because I donated a lot. They want to motivate me to donate more. In addition, I'm one of the Chinese entrepreneurs with the most social positions…party representative, member of the CPPCC Standing Committee, president of All-China Federation of Industry and Commerce and many other commissions, etc. Of course, I try to talk with college students as much as I can. I'd like to take this opportunity to suggest to students here today who are interested in starting their own businesses that they should apply to the Ying Foundation. The foundation has over 20 entrepreneurship service centers across the country. They hire start-up entrepreneurs with five to ten years of experience to offer guidance as supervisors, and they can assess your business proposals. The foundation provides everyone with one million yuan of funding, free of interest, but you need to repay it. It supports and encourages young people to start their own businesses.

Q: I'm from Tsinghua University Chinese Entrepreneurs Camp. I have two questions. First, as both Wanda Cinemas and Wanda Real Estate are applying for IPOs, could you share with us the latest progress? Second, regarding a recent report saying that there is still room for the Chinese real estate market to drop further by 20%, what's your opinion about the real estate industry in China in the near future?

Wang Jianlin: We do have two companies applying for IPOs, but in view of the government's regulation of the real estate market, there may be difficulties in listing Wanda's commercial property business.

Wanda cinemas are a cultural business, so I personally think that it will be slightly easier. We decided to launch the IPO projects, not because we need to increase cash flow or I need them myself, but for the sake of small shareholders that have worked with me over the years. Last year, I distributed more than five billion yuan worth of shares to the senior managers. In addition, once the companies are listed, more shares will be offered to senior managers above a certain level. I believe, as long as the companies are of good quality, an IPO is just a matter of time. If our applications are rejected this year, we'll apply again next year and the year after.

As to your second question, if I say there's no more room for further price reduction, some of you might say that it's just me boasting about my own business, but I would be a liar if I said there is room for further reduction. Indeed, housing prices in China have been affected by government regulation, but price reductions have been slow because the housing price is made up of many rigid costs, including the cost of land, building materials, labor and taxes, which are rising. It would be unrealistic to expect a sharp fall in the housing price as these costs keep increasing. The housing price will fall, and profits of property developers will be lowered to a reasonable level. This is possible. But that's about the limit. I must say that the reality is always different from what people wish to see.

Q: First, how would you describe government-business relations in China today? And how would you describe the ideal relationship between the government and entrepreneurs and private companies? Second, as many of the audience are college students and young people, and your child is perhaps about the same age as us, as a father, could you share with us your experience in educating your child?

Wang Jianlin: This sounds very interesting. Let's talk about government-business relations first. Business is business, and politics is politics. Europe and the U.S. may have the best government-business relations, but it would be difficult for China at the time being because the Chinese economy is dominated by the government. The government dominates everything and makes the most crucial decisions.

If a businessman detaches himself completely from the government, I think that's not right either. They say businessmen should "stay close to the government but away from politics." I think that's a wise attitude. Entrepreneurs should take a proactive stance in coping with government officials, but one should not rely on power-for-money deals. Not every company can copy Wanda's model – doing business completely by selecting from government invitations.

To answer your second question, my son is 24 years old. He's running his own business. Because I'm a busy man, I don't have any experience to share about children's education. I might be a strict father. Family education is not like business, and I don't have any experience to talk about. My requirements for my son…from the bottom of my heart I hope that he will be hardworking, dedicated to his work and kind-hearted, so I can let him succeed to my position in the future. Wanda is not a family business, and none of my relatives have worked in the company so far. I don't have to pass it on to my son. I've drawn up a schedule for myself, that is, by the time I retire in 2020, Wanda's revenue will have reached 500-600 billion yuan with several hundreds of thousands of employees. If my son has the ability, I'll let him take over the company. If not and I force him to accept it, I'd be ruining his life. More importantly, it would be irresponsible for the employees. So I think…let him do whatever he's capable of, and if he's not suitable, I can always hire professional managers.

Q: I'm from Hilton Hotel Asia Pacific. Ten of the thirty 5-star Hilton Hotels in China are owned by Wanda, and Wanda is our largest property owner in China. As Hilton will build 100 new 5-star hotels in China in the next three years, will Wanda continue to be our largest property owner? And what's your plan in terms of Wanda hotel branding?

Wang Jianlin: We'll definitely continue cooperating with Hilton in the future. Resorts developed by Wanda in Sanya, Changbai Mountain, Xishuangbanna, etc. have over a dozen hotels in each location, and some of them are Hilton hotels. Also there'll be cooperation opportunities between us in other cities across China. As to our own hotel brand, Wanda has just set up its own 5-star hotel management company. By the end of the year, we'll have 40 partner hotels, with dozens more under construction. At the current rate, we'll have more than 100 5-star hotels by 2020. If we still rely on external companies for hotel management after we've built the 100th hotel, I'd be worried that future Wanda generations may question our inability to take on the minor challenge of managing hotels by ourselves. Therefore, we decided to operate hotels by ourselves and through delegated management as well. Besides, leaders from the central government have talked with me several times. They told me that China needed to have its own luxury hotel brand, and they hoped it would be Wanda. There are no other companies capable of opening over a dozen luxury hotels every year. Hotels are the biggest luxury good in the world today. If Wanda does not dare to do it, no one else can! You see, we're running the hotel business not purely for the sake of the company alone, we also need to fulfill our responsibilities to the Chinese nation. Through our hard work in the next five or ten years, we'll create a luxury hotel brand with at least a leading position in the regional market in Asia. Needless to say, this does not compromise our partnership plans with other companies.

Q: I'm a PhD student from the School of Public Policy and Management, Tsinghua University. Your success story is very inspiring. What are your life goals or what is your lifelong pursuit that you aspire to?

Wang Jianlin: Many years ago, I said…that Mr. Michael Saul Dell, founder of Dell Inc. once observed that the biggest achievement of his life was that he created a great organization. My lifelong goal is to build a great organization in the world. It should continue to be a great organization after I pass it on to future generations. This is the goal of my life. That's why I work so hard now. I was not as hard working and ambitious ten years ago. The goal of my life has changed as the company has grown. If I didn't live in a large country like China, if my company didn't have assets worth tens or billions or even a hundred billion yuan and aspire to be a Fortune 500, Fortune 100 company…If I only had 100 million yuan, it would all be nothing but wishful thinking. But now, Wanda has the necessary foundation and the potential, and we only need to put in more hard work, energy and time, and my ambitions will come true. We're presented with a historic opportunity. We can't waste it. I'm not saying that everyone should have such ambitions. It's possible for us to be the best and biggest in the world. My lifetime ambition is to create a Chinese enterprise that is respected by everyone in the world, to prove that the Chinese people are as good as or even better than Westerners.

Q: I work in the real estate business. I wanted to ask what Wanda's advantages and strategy are in terms of human resources to support its continuous expansion of the commercial property business, industry restructuring and sustained innovations. Many companies face the issue of staff loss as a side effect of business transformation. How does Wanda address this challenge?

Wang Jianlin: Human resources are the biggest development bottleneck confronting Wanda. This is what constrains our development across all business segments. First of all, we've been expanding very rapidly. We recruited 15,700 new employees last year, and 20,000 this year. Second, all of our businesses are of an innovative nature. Commercial properties, high-end hotels, cultural businesses, tourism and resorts…There doesn't exist any model in China that we can learn from. It gives our human resources department such a headache. That's why we place a lot of emphasis on training and invest more than 100 million yuan in training each year. Three years ago, we bought a piece of land of over 13 hectares in Langfang and invested 780 million yuan to build a company college of the highest standard in China. It's called Wanda Institute and opened last year. Approximately 10,000 students are trained there every year. Most of them are management staff above the level of department managers. In addition, we pay headhunters tens of millions of yuan every year to obtain qualified professionals that we need. Another thing is internal staff promotion. We prioritize training of existing employees. Training has become one of the ingredients that makes up Wanda's competitiveness.

We open more than 20 plazas and 10-15 5-star hotels every year. Actually, we can open 30 or even more based on financial capacity and development speed. Our constraints come from human resources rather than funding. For example, if we open 20 plazas, we need 20 commercial property management companies, 20 management teams, 20 top-level leaders supported by 70-80 assistant managers; we also need 20 department store management teams, 30-40 cinema management teams and KTV teams. These are our development constraints. Every year, we have to assess the maximum capacity of our management companies, and how many new teams we need to set up. I hope that Wanda Institute can tackle this issue in about five years.

Q: I'm also in the commercial property business. We've been learning from the Wanda model, but our company is pretty small. We copy the Wanda model and apply it in tier-three, four or even five cities. Do you mind us doing this? We developed a gold and jewelry park for the cultural and creative industry in Beijing and plan to reproduce it in provincial capitals based on the same model. Could I have your opinions about our model?

Wang Jianlin: All enterprises learn from each other. We set a target last year, that is, teaching materials would be sorted and be made available to the public nationwide next year, in addition to internal use by Wanda Institute. We've seen many good projects in China gone to waste. They (the developers) purchased the land but had difficulties in attracting tenants. I hope to share professional expertise with you. Wanda has entered commercial property markets in tier-three cities.

To answer your second question, as people's spending power increases, consumption of gold, jewelry and accessories will increase – that's for sure. No question about it. Many people visit Hong Kong to buy gold and jewelry, which means nothing is wrong with this business, but if you want to reproduce the model on a nationwide scale, you'll face the issue of tenant attraction. How many jewelry companies have signed cooperation agreements with you? This will dictate the scalability of your business model. If you had more than 100 or hundreds of partners, your business would be highly scalable, but if you plan to find tenants after the construction is completed, you must be careful about it.

Q: I got to know you and Wanda after I heard about your ventures in the football business. Football leagues in Japan and South Korea, for example, are fully market-oriented with professional players, and it's proven useful to boost the quality of their football teams. If football in China is to be improved, shouldn't we turn the Chinese football league into a truly professional one and run it as a fully market-based business?

Wang Jianlin: Wanda offered support again to China's football league last year. Now that I'm a supporter of the football association, our national team and the league, it'd be inappropriate for me to criticize them here. So regrettably, I can't tell you what I think about this matter. How do we improve the quality of the football league in China is even more difficult. China has achieved remarkable economic growth. We've tackled virtually all problems, but football is the only exception. In China, football and the stock markets are the toughest challenges to overcome,so don't ask me this.

Chapter Five

Internationalization

Wanda's Rapid Growth

8 September, 2012 – A speech at Harvard University

September 8 (U.S.A. time), Wang Jianlin visited Harvard University with a group of Wanda colleagues. He delivered a speech of over an hour and answered questions from the audience. His speech touched upon the four major moves that Wanda has implemented over the course of its development and the reasons behind Wanda's rapid development.

I'm thrilled to bits to be able to speak here today, as I've always held Harvard in awe as a sacred place venerated by people all around the world. There's still a big gap between Wanda and the world's top ranking companies. We'll continue with our hard work and won't slacken our efforts in the slightest. Today, I'd like to take this opportunity to share with you my experience as an entrepreneur.

I. The four major moves

Wanda was founded in 1988. We completed license registration with borrowed money. In those days, to set up a real estate company required one million yuan of registered capital. I borrowed the money, and the loan had to be supported by a guarantor. The guarantor took half a million away, so we were left with just half a million. Even worse, the lender asked me to repay the loan in five years, on top of 25% interest to be paid every year. These were very tough terms, but were it not for the loan that year to pay for our registered capital, Wanda might have disappeared a long time ago. The company has grown rapidly in the past years, mainly on account of our ability to innovate. We have implemented four major moves during the development history of Wanda.

1. Nationwide-scale business expansion

The first move was for Wanda to go beyond the local market in Dalian, building up a business presence in cities across China. The company was founded in 1988, and we went outside Dalian to Guangzhou in 1992. We were the first property developer in China to pioneer cross-regional project development. At that time, the government did not allow private companies to set up branches outside their own local administrative divisions. We were confronted with numerous difficulties. We planned to develop properties in Guangzhou but were not allowed to register companies there. Most people would back out seeing the policy barriers, but I believed in what Chairman Mao once said, "Nothing is difficult to the man who will try." I give it a try even though there were policy barriers! I found some local companies in Guangzhou to see who would lend us the license. At last, a local company, SOCT Real Estate, registered a branch company for us, and we agreed to pay them two million yuan a year in exchange. It worked. It was in Guangzhou that Wanda started cross-regional development. It has been simply unstoppable ever since. As of the end of this year, Wanda will have invested in more than 90 Chinese cities, making us a leading real estate developer with the largest cross-regional business presence in the country. Through nationwide development, Wanda grew from an obscure local company into a large national enterprise.

2. Commercial properties

The second move concerned our entry into the commercial property business. Up to 2000, we mainly focused on housing properties and made a lot of money out of it. So why did we decide to switch to real estate? It's because I was touched by the tragedies that befell two of our employees who had worked with me ever since the start of the company. One of them was diagnosed with cancer and the other with liver disease. As private companies didn't have any medical or pension insurance at that time, it was up to the company to decide whether or not to cover medical treatment for the employees, i.e. if it had enough money and was willing to pay. I decided to pay their medical costs. It cost the company over three million yuan in total. I couldn't help thinking that Wanda was still young. What would we do when we had tens of thousands of employees 20 years later, many of whom would be old, retired, and need medical expense coverage?

Residential property development is characterized by unstable cash flow – cash flow is good only when there are developed properties for sale, but it disappears once the properties are sold out and the next land acquisition-project development cycle begins. Besides, the real estate industry in China is frequently affected by government regulations, causing even greater fluctuations in cash flow. I worried that sticking to housing properties, in extreme cases, might threaten the company's survival and the lives of our employees. We tried many different things to ensure a stable cash flow. We tried manufacturing and our products included OTIS, a well-known elevator brand in China, transformers and pharmaceuticals as well as supermarkets and foreign trade. In 2000, we decided to develop commercial properties as the pillar business of Wanda. Before the decision was made, we debated internally about it for two to three years. We felt that commercial property development would involve construction and tenant attraction. At least we knew everything about the first part, so we went all out for it. After a few years we got the hang of it, and our business model matured too. It was a transformational process, in which our attitude changed from reactive to active, from an unconscious action to self-conscious development.

Today, Wanda operates 13 million square meters of commercial properties, ranking it number 3 in the world. We have 20 million square meters of commercial properties under construction. Moreover, our development has been very fast, with four million square meters of properties opening every year. By 2015, Wanda will have grown into the largest commercial property developer in the world. Our success is partly attributable to our dedication over the years, and partly thanks to the vast market, huge population and enormous total consumption in China.

We entered the high-end hotel business and experimented with the first few projects. We found that by combining hotels with business, office buildings, apartments, etc. our products became more popular among the consumers. So we decided to develop future projects based on this model. Almost all shopping centers we developed have a 5-star hotel. As a result, Wanda became the world's largest owner of 5-star hotel properties within a few years. We now own 38 hotels in operation, in addition to another 30 hotels currently under construction.

The Wanda model for commercial property development has been warmly received by local governments all around China. Unlike the U.S. where land can be traded freely, land in China can only be purchased from the government. As we receive invitations for local project development from an increasing number of governments, Wanda is gradually now moving into the driving seat during negotiations, and our bargaining power has increased. The result is that we can obtain land at a much lower price than our competitors. The ratio of the number of project invitations we receive and that of projects we actually develop is 3:1 to 4:1. We have the right to choose clients, which translates into higher profits.

3. Culture and tourism

The third move was our embarkation on cultural and tourism businesses. We started operating cinemas as early as 2003, because we needed to include cinemas in Wanda's shopping malls. At first, we talked with Time Warner for cooperation, but it didn't work out due to reasons on both sides. Firstly, it was agreed during the WTO talks between China and the U.S. that foreign companies could not be the controlling shareholders of Chinese cinemas, and Time Warner didn't want to be the minority shareholder. Secondly, Time Warner misjudged the Chinese movie market – the gross box office in China was no more than US$100 million, and they thought that the investment was not worth it. We had to look for partners in China. Back then all local cinemas belonged to state-owned media groups. We talked with them in Shanghai, Jiangsu, Guangdong and Beijing, proposing that they operate the cinemas with Wanda as the property owner. As they were all governmental organizations and were not very interested in boosting profit, the negotiations were all broken off in the end.

An interesting episode back then occurred when the then president of the Shanghai Media Group, a very creative man, thought the cooperation was a good deal for his company. We signed an agreement with him, and he paid us the deposit. However, a new president replaced him half a year later, and the new president was against the deal and refused to implement the agreement. We had ten new stores due to open soon, so we had to run the cinemas ourselves. As it happened, the Chinese movie market started to take off in 2005 and grew over 30% every year thereafter. China's gross box office this year will exceed 16 billion yuan. If the Chinese market continues to grow by 25% every year, it's poised to take over North America as the world's largest movie market in 2018.

Apart from cinemas, Wanda entered many other cultural businesses. For example, as part of our deployment for performing arts, we invested 10 billion yuan in acquiring the production team of the famous "Le Rêve– The Dream." They will help us create five world-class performance shows in China. Wanda Movie Park will launch its first project in Wuhan in 2014. Unlike Disney and Universal Studios whose amusement parks only have comparatively few features, the Wanda Movie Park in Wuhan features six themes, all of which are developed based on Chinese legends and Chinese images.

Our cultural businesses have achieved considerable growth, so we set up a group for the cultural industry. Cultural businesses are now defined as a pillar industry for Wanda. This year, we rank among the top 40 cultural companies globally, in terms of revenue. By 2016, our cultural businesses will yield revenue of 40 billion yuan, and our ranking will rise to the top 20. By 2020, cultural business revenue will increase to 80 billion yuan, and the ranking will move up to within the top 10.

Wanda started investing in tourism businesses in 2008. Our first project was Changbaishan International Resort. The resort measures 22 square kilometers and cost us 20 billion yuan. It's now in operation and has been warmly received by the market, much better than what we had expected. The Wanda resort in Xishuangbanna is under construction. In designing the projects, we challenged traditional resort theories by incorporating and highlighting cultural and business elements such as luxury hotels, "tourists' towns" and theatres in every resort project.

4. Transnational development

Our fourth move was transnational development. Why is transnational development necessary? First, growing at the current rate, Wanda's assets will total 280 billion yuan this year, with our annual revenue hitting 145 billion. Our company is already big enough, but if we stay in China, Wanda will remain a national business no matter how much bigger we grow. To make Wanda a major international brand, we must go beyond China. Second, we need to spread risks and can't have all the eggs in the same basket. We announced the ten-year strategic program earlier this year and plan to establish Wanda as a world-class enterprise in ten years. At present, there are over 70 Chinese companies included in Fortune's top500 companies in the world, but only three or four of them are private enterprises. Wanda wants to prove with its performance results that private Chinese companies are also capable of achieving sound and rapid development, without preferential policies offered by the state.

Our first move in transnational development was the acquisition of AMC Cinemas in the U.S. Additionally, we're contacting the six largest American film production companies to strengthen our cooperation ties with them in terms of content. Wanda is not internationalizing for internationalization's sake, and the AMC deal is not purely motivated by the need for business expansion. Instead, while we scale up our business presence, we make sure that profits are maintained at a healthy level. Negotiations about the acquisition lasted for more than two years. We learned many lessons during this period. We found that many large American companies were owned by small shareholders and foundations, and none of them are the real company owner. All of them were driven by short-term profit. Consequently, the companies lacked strategic planning for long-term development. Therefore, as long as Wanda manages to restrain itself from focusing on short-term gains and sustain temporary losses, we'll benefit from the long-term opportunities in the U.S. and Europe.

II. Reasons behind Wanda's rapid growth

Wanda's rapid development is mainly attributable to the following reasons:

1. An advanced business model

There are different types of business innovation such as technical, management and cultural. Of these, innovation of the business model is one of the most important factors. I always believed that the value of business model innovation is far greater than that of technical and management innovations. For example, everyone knows how to sell coffee, but Starbucks redesigned the coffee-making process, innovated the business model and became a successful chain business. Other similar examples include McDonald's and KFC. I'm strongly opposed to the argument that high-tech, new energy and new materials are the only hopes, and no other businesses can possibly compete with them. It seems to me that no matter whether you are in a traditional or an emerging industry, as long as you're capable of innovating the existing business model, you can reap super profits. This way, your business will enjoy a longer life cycle because traditional industries can last hundreds of years. By contrast, the so-called "advanced" businesses do not necessarily last long.

2. High standard information management

Wanda set up an information management center many years ago to attract talent in China and from abroad. We have developed and manage our own information system. Wanda is one of the most prolific developers of patented management software and relevant intellectual properties in China – we were granted nearly 20 national patents and intellectual properties last year alone. Wanda is best-known for its modular management model, where the entire commercial property development process is divided into nearly 400 segments in chronological sequence, with strict regulations as to the specific tasks to be performed by relevant departments in each segment. The segments are further divided into three tiers, corresponding to different management levels. For example, presidents are only responsible for tier-one segments, vice presidents for tier-two segments, and project companies for tier-three segments. A modular management software is then developed based on the regulations so that in November of each year, specific day-to-day tasks planned for every individual unit and employee for the following year can be entered into the system. Performance appraisal is automatically carried out by the information system. If a given employee fails to complete the scheduled progress by the preset deadline, the "yellow light" turns on by way of warning; if s/he fails to catch up within the time limit, the "red light" goes on. Once this happens, related managers will be penalized, and the penalties are connected with their income. All thanks to the modular management system, everything at Wanda has been progressing in an "intense but orderly manner" despite the dramatic development of the company during the past two decades.

Strong execution and effective discipline are the other main reasons behind Wanda's rapid growth. There are no office politics at Wanda, and I don't have any relatives working in the company. All these factors combined enabled Wanda to develop at a dramatic pace. We're not the only company that is illustrative of the rapid growth of the Chinese economy. Rather, there are many other private companies like Wanda in China, and a large number of high quality private Chinese companies will emerge as China's economy continues to develop. They will all become world-class enterprises. Ten years ago, 197 of the Fortune 500 companies were based in the U.S. and only seven were from China. In 2011, there were 145 American companies and 74 Chinese companies included in the Fortune 500 list. At this rate, China and the U.S. will have about 100 companies each listed, or China may even outnumber the U.S. Whether Americans acknowledge this or not, whether they like it or not, this is the trend. In light of the strong complementary economic connections between China and the U.S., I believe nothing will separate the two countries. And Chinese companies, such as Wanda will increasingly go to the U.S. for development.

Q&A

Q: The acquisition of AMC is Wanda's first M&A deal overseas, so have you encountered any unanticipated difficulties? At the price of US$2.6 billion, would you say it's too expensive or a real bargain?

Wang Jianlin: It has been a process of trial and error. We talked with the shareholders at first but changed the plan to talking with the management first because a stable management team is the key. Otherwise, even if we had successfully closed the deal, it would have been a waste of money if all the people were gone. Talking with the management was anything but easy. The AMC managers received many interested buyers during the past ten years, and Wanda was just another one for them at first. We needed to convince them that Wanda would benefit the company's development over the long term. We started talking with the shareholders after negotiations with the management were almost done.

Is US$2.6 billion too expensive? Let's do the number crunching. First, AMC carries several hundred million dollars on the book; second, AMC holds equity shares worth more than US$200 million in market cap in the largest American cinema advertising company. The price comes down to about US$2 billion after deducting these two items, and then each cinema screen is worth an average of three million yuan. Actually, building a movie theatre in the U.S. costs more than three million; even in China, the actual cost is four million yuan. With this cost breakdown, we think the deal is reasonably priced. But, of course, AMC was in the third year of loss making. If it went on like that forever, being cheap alone wouldn't make the deal work. We had to figure out a way to turn it around. For this reason, we made an institutional arrangement that Wanda would not take part in AMC's management directly. We only assigned one of our managers to work there. We signed a long-term agreement with the management, and offered them a moderate pay raise. We set up an incentive scheme, that is, as long as they could turn the company around, the management would get 10% of the profit. Besides, in principle, Wanda won't take away the money earned. Instead, it will be re-invested in the U.S. market. After the deal, Wanda allocated US$500 million to AMC for cinema renovation.

We expected that the renovations would lead to an increase in profit within a few years. The increased profit would be insufficient to raise a lot of money after listing on the U.S. capital market, but the earnings ratio may look good on the Chinese market. This institutional change boosted the company's performance. The management has told me that it would show a profit this year.

Q: What are the differences between the cultural industries in China and the U.S.?

Wang Jianlin: From the economic perspective, the gap between the two countries has become smaller and smaller. China's GDP will exceed that of the U.S. within the next ten years. If we convert it to purchasing power parity (PPP), it may come even sooner. But there's a bigger gap between the Chinese and American cultural industries. Even after China overtakes the U.S. in terms of GDP, cultural businesses in China would still be rather lagging behind their American counterparts. For example, while developing the six technology entertainment themes for Wanda's movie park in Wuhan, we needed to produce a 3-D promo. A Chinese designer would typically show the location, entertainment activities, etc. of the park. We hired an American team to produce the video, and we saw the difference the first time we watched their work. The video showed a family of three in the house; the mother was cooking, and the father was reading a book with the daughter. As they opened the book, images of the 4-D, 5-D, flight and interactive cinemas appeared. The father and the daughter found it very interesting and started talking about the park full of passion. The mother came out from the kitchen and asked, "What are you talking about?" He told her it was a movie park being built in Wuhan, and they flipped through the book. When they finished reading the book, the daughter said, "This was so much fun. When will it open?" The answer was "in 2014." The concept was pretty simple, but it presents details of the project in a way that is very easy to understand for the viewers, so I would say that the biggest difference between Chinese and American cultural industries lies in creative thinking, rather than technical production.

Q: Wanda Plazas in Shanghai and Beijing give people the impression that they're more or less the same. If some better consumption models emerge in China, say, ten years later, won't Wanda Plaza be outdated?

Wang Jianlin: It's both right and wrong to say that different Wanda Plazas are similar to each other. It's correct in the sense that every Wanda Plaza is a complex including a department store, a supermarket, a cinema and restaurants, and interior decorations are not dramatically different. In Chinese we say, "the experts see the nature of things, while the laymen can only see the superficial phenomena". In the eyes of an expert, restaurants in one Wanda Plaza are totally different from the others, because the local food cultures are different in different places. It is a rule at Wanda that opening any plaza must be preceded with thorough research into the local catering market. At least 20 of the top 30 local catering brands must be introduced. Therefore, the catering brands in a given Wanda Plaza are very different from those found in other Wanda Plazas. Even clothing brands are different from city to city.

As to what happens ten years later, making adjustments is a fundamental law in commerce. There are two major rounds of adjustments every year. We call them spring adjustment and autumn adjustment. Agreements signed between Wanda Plazas and our tenants typically last three years; the longest of which is no more than five years because we need to make adjustments in the future. Therefore, we don't need to worry about what happens ten years later, as adjustments and adaptions are constantly made to Wanda Plazas. Even when it's impossible to adjust an existing plaza, we can always tear it down and rebuild it. In China, it's much cheaper to rebuild a property than to purchase land and develop a new one from scratch.

Q: My question is will Wanda move its own managers to the U.S. to manage the company or hire Chinese people who have lived in the U.S. for a long time and let them do it?

Wang Jianlin: Americans are our first choice. One thing's for sure – I won't send many Chinese managers to the U.S. because even if they speak good English, they're no match for local Americans in terms of their knowledge about the local markets. Our second choice would be Chinese people living in relevant American cities. For example, for a project located in Washington DC, I won't choose Chinese managers living in Los Angeles to manage it. The managers must be natives of the cities where the projects are located. Wanda only sent one of its people to AMC – a contact person without a senior position, just the liaison officer. Talent localization is the general trend in the world. Some of the Fortune 500 companies with Chinese branches assigned many managers from their headquarters to China, and none of them performed very well. By the same token, it won't work if we send many Chinese managers over to manage our American branch.

Q: We seldom see Wanda's properties at any prime business locations in Beijing or Shanghai. Could you tell us why?

Wang Jianlin: First, Wanda Plazas are positioned as shopping facilities for fashion products, not luxury goods, so only very few of our properties are developed at prime locations. It's cheaper to acquire land at locations that are further away from the city center. However, due to our brand advantage and high growth potential, we always manage to obtain relatively high rental income. From a financial perspective, it doesn't make sense for us to choose the central locations. Second, it's not just because Wanda doesn't want to acquire land at prime locations, but during the early years of China's economic reforms, foreign investors and those from Hong Kong had more capital, and they bought a lot of the land in central locations. There's no more land left for us even if we wanted, such as Nanjing Road in Shanghai or Wangfujing in Beijing. In other words, we have to look for opportunities in new areas.

Wanda will open a top luxury store in Wuhan and Changsha next year. In particular, the Wanda Plaza on Han Street in Wuhan has the very best architectural design, interior design and tenant resources among all luxury shopping malls in the world! Business is business. The fact that Wanda has developed several shopping malls like that attests to our ability to develop luxury stores. We can make them even better. This is enough. After all, commerce is meant to make money.

Q: Wanda's acquisition of the AMC marks major progress for the internationalization of Chinese cultural businesses. Have there been any legal challenges encountered during the process?

Wang Jianlin: To be honest, our biggest concern about the acquisition is the security assessment by the American government. According to U.S. law, all foreign companies applying to invest in the U.S. must pass the security assessment. It's an optional requirement, but they can shut down a company even if it's been in business for 50 years, as soon as a security violation has been identified. Hence, we had to apply for a security assessment, but as it turned out, our worries were unnecessary. First, we didn't acquire any sensitive businesses such as national defense or energy. Second, Wanda is a genuine private company, so we got the approvals from the Department of Commerce and the Department of Homeland Security within one month, half a month earlier than approvals from the Chinese government.

Q: The growth of the Chinese economy has slowed down since the beginning of this year. Does this mean that something's wrong with the Chinese economy? Will the high growth continue?

Wang Jianlin: China's economic growth will remain above 8% at least for the next 15-20 years, because the main drivers have not disappeared. First, the urbanization process has not yet come to an end. The urbanization rate in China is only 51% at present, and the actual urbanization rate, including towns and cities, is merely about 40%. It is laid down in the national strategy that the urbanization rate will increase by 0.8-1% every year, meaning 10-13 million people will migrate to the cities every year. Urbanization in China will generate enormous demand, big enough to support the relatively fast growth of the Chinese economy for another 15-20 years. The growth will slow down only after 70-80% of the Chinese population is urbanized. The slowdown in China's economic growth in the last couple of years was not caused by the global economic downturn, but rather it was because China decided to restructure the economy and curb the real estate sector on its own initiative. Second, China is currently in the middle of the industrialization process, which has not yet ended. There's still plenty of room for improvement in terms of per capita highway and high-speed railway ownership and steel consumption in China.

Q: What were the challenges and risks facing Wanda when you decided to acquire a company that had been making losses for several years?

Wang Jianlin: An old Chinese saying goes, "seek wealth in danger." If everyone thinks something will be successful, never touch it! Success is when you drive a business to success when only a few people believe that the business is the right thing to do. This is the only way to make more profit. As for the AMC deal, we'd wanted to give it a try regardless of the results. It was not a question of the risks involved. If there were no risks, what would we need enterprises for? It's actually the risks and cha lenges that give people a sense of fulfillment, success and happiness. More pain brings more happiness. I believe that Wanda can turn risks into profit. After the acquisition, we didn't make any major changes to AMC. What we did is we increased its capital and lowered the debt ratio to make financing easier for the company. AMC has Wanda's backing, and we promised that we'd never sell the business. Banks in China and the states alike are willing to do business with Wanda. AMC's bond prices rose immediately after the acquisition. Second, Wanda created a mechanism for the AMC management, pledging extra bonuses for the managers if they managed to make the company a profitable business; the profits will be kept in the U.S. for continuous investment. The result is that the company will make a turnaround after having made losses in the past three years. However, at the end of the day, everything I said here today needs to be proven in the next three years. The company may be successful or unsuccessful, but even if it fails, it won't cause any major risks given Wanda's financial strength today.

Q: Running a company like yours involves numerous interactions with the government. What are the risks and challenges that you face because of such interactions?

Wang Jianlin: Government-business relations are very complicated in China. It's even more difficult than completing a PhD course at Harvard. An American official working in China once told me that he was impressed more than anything else by the ability of successful private entrepreneurs in China. It's difficult to develop a successful private company of scale in China. It takes several times the time, energy, etc. that would have been required of an American to run a successful business in the U.S. The Chinese economy and the Asian economies in general are dominated by the government, and no one can work around government-business relations. My theory is to "stay close to the government but away from politics." A company cannot be successful if it ignores the government altogether, and this is true in the U.S. as well. Business people need to draw a line between maintaining a close connection with the government and doing something with the government that would cause permanent harm to themselves.

Q: In your opinion, what are the key factors for starting a successful business in China? Which areas merit particular attention?

Wang Jianlin: Unfortunately, the Chinese market has become a tougher place than it was ten years ago because in the past competition only came from state-owned enterprises, but today a large number of private companies have grown up as strong competitors, leaving little room for others, small businesses in particular. That said, China still has more opportunities than the U.S., and it's still easier to start a successful business in China.

Wanda started as a small company. During the first five years, I experienced a lot of discrimination and people giving me cold-eyed stares, so I'm very sympathetic about thedifficulties small businesses face. All of my CPPCC proposals and speeches revolve around private enterprises. I proposed exempting small businesses from taxes, offering them low-interest loans and so on and so forth. I've also decided to start a foundation for young entrepreneurs next year. According to a report that I read, fewer than 1% of Chinese university students started their own business in 2011. I'm very worried that a generation gap may occur among Chinese entrepreneurs, private business owners in particular. There are already signs of this actually. Most active entrepreneurs in China today are of a senior age. We need the younger generations, people in their20s or 30s, to be prepared to be our successors.

If so, China would stand a better chance of success, so I'm willing to support young entrepreneurs.

As for Chinese people returning to China from abroad to set up new businesses, I think the most important thing for them is to be realistic. They need to be ready to swallow their pride. Consumer goods are the best place to start a new business in China because the Chinese consumer market is huge, but if you have patents and are innovative, you may venture into technology or IT businesses. According to the government's plan, by 2015, the size of the consumer market in China will be double that of 2010, with another two-fold increase expected before 2020, by which time the market volume will have reached over a dozen trillion dollars, making China the largest consumer market in the world. Therefore, it's advisable to focus your business on consumer goods, food or clothing. I think they stand a pretty good chance of success.

Q: Wanda started as a commercial property developer, so why did you choose the cultural business rather than commercial properties for your first move in the overseas market?

Wang Jianlin: Real estate anywhere is always a business in great need of localization. It involves complex development processes that can't be standardized. Every single project must be individually designed. For this reason, Wanda won't make large-scale expansions into any overseas real estate markets. Even if we invested in a couple of projects, they would only be experiments. We chose to start with the cultural business for overseas expansion, and it was more by chance than design. AMC happened to be looking for a takeover deal, and I was interested. It all happened by coincidence. I'm interested in acquiring hotel management companies in the U.S. and have talked with many companies, but it turns out to be difficult as it appeared so far. Which business goes out first is just the luck of the draw.

Q: What was your bottom line for the AMC acquisition? What was the worst scenario in your plan, and what did you do to prevent it from happening?

Wang Jianlin: Transnational acquisitions are never easy, but it's an obstacle every company must surpass if it's to become internationalized. It's virtually impossible to scale up a business by relying on organic growth alone. None of the Fortune 500 companies managed to grow to the size that they have today without M&A, but once we decided to go with the acquisition deal, we started making thorough preparations for it. First, we compared our cash flow against the losses if the business failed. In other words, whether or not we could sustain such losses? If so, we'd proceed. Otherwise, we'd have dropped it. Second, we assessed the possible outcomes of the acquisition. We engaged external teams to do technical analyses, and hired several of them. Then, in-depth discussions were carried out with the target company, and the decision was made only after the results of external assessments matched those provided by the target company and our own assessments. In short, we needed to make sure that we had enough resources to sustain the potential losses through thorough technical assessments.

Q: Do American students or American companies have any advantages if they venture into the Chinese market?

Wang Jianlin: I once said in a speech that "a degree from Tsinghua or Peking University can't beat having guts." Now I'd like to change it to "a degree from Harvard or Yale can't beat having guts". Opportunities arise when you struggle your way up to success. They can't be calculated. To create a successful business you'll need to have guts and an enterprising spirit. From my own experience and that of many successful businessmen I've met, the biggest lesson we learned is that the enterprising spirit is the first thing it takes to start a successful business. As the old Chinese saying goes, "seek wealth in danger." If you want to set up a new business, you've got to give it a try no matter how big or small your chances are that it will be a success. If a business is bound to be successful…it can't be that easy. If all of your friends tell you that something is worth a try, don't touch it; if only three of your friends tell you that something is a good business, and all the rest doubt it, you may give it a try. You may lose, but you can start afresh. After all, you've got age on your side. I'm not saying that you can do whatever you like blindly. It'd be advisable to start with something small that doesn't require heavy investments, as an experiment. My advice is: be bold – it helps more than anything else. What is entrepreneurship? It involves two things: one is innovation, or the enterprising spirit, and the other is perseverance. All successful entrepreneurs, especially the great ones, tend to be maniacs. They believe in their stories and believe that they will succeed even after the umpteenth failure. Without perseverance, no one could be successful.

Chapter Six

Entertainment

Wanda's Cultural Industry

21 March, 2012 – Shanghai Cultural Industry Development Lecture Course

Today, I would like to introduce Wanda's cultural industry to you. In 2006 Wanda set foot in the cultural industry and as of now it has been involved in the cultural tourism city, the film industry, performing arts, film technology entertainment, theme parks, children's entertainment chains, wholesale KTV chains, newspapers, and art collections, among other fields. In 2012 the Cultural Industry Group was incorporated in Beijing, and the cultural industry's revenue surpassed 10 billion yuan. In 2013 the revenue was 25.5 billion yuan, and it was announced by the Central Propaganda Department that the Cultural Industry Group was the first among the top 30 national cultural industries. This year Wanda Cultural Group's revenue target is 32 billion yuan, but it is estimated that we will beat this. Wanda Cultural Industry's revenue has annual growth of the order of magnitude of 10 billion yuan and our target is to enter the world's top ten cultural enterprises by 2020 with 80 billion yuan in revenue. How does Wanda develop its cultural industry? I will give you an introduction to four aspects:

I. Why the cultural industry?

1. Transform and Upgrade Requirements

When Wanda was established in Dalian, the main business was real estate, and during 27 years of existence, four big changes have occurred. Each was an active transformation. The first was in 1993 with cross-regional development from Dalian to Guangzhou. Later development moved throughout the whole country, and Wanda was the nation's first private enterprise to develop inter-regionally. In 2000, Wanda transitioned from residential to immovable property and entered the cultural industry in 2006. In 2012, Wanda implemented transnational development. Entering the cultural industry was essential to Wanda's transformation and upgrade.

Wanda's earliest cultural industry was cinema. Because cinema was a very important consumer experience in a Wanda Plaza, it was a format that had to be configured at all Wanda Plazas. At that time Wanda signed a strategic cooperation agreement with SVA (Group) Co., Ltd. They were willing to follow Wanda's development and manage where cinemas were built. Later SVA Group's leader was replaced, and the new leader did not think the cooperation had prospects and terminated the contract. Then Wanda, already with a dozen cinemas open or soon to open, had to take over for itself. You could say that Wanda entered the cultural industry and was driven to desperate action. It never expected to become the world's number one cinema chain by accident, but Wanda has undertaken, of its own accord, this whole-scale transformation towards the cultural industry. It has become fully culturally conscious, and it has expanded into many areas of the cultural industry.

2. Establishing a New Competitive Advantage

In business, no matter the industry, the strategy, or the operations, the ultimate goal is to establish a core competitive advantage and to obtain greater profits. Back in 1993, when Wanda was in Dalian, revenue had already surpassed two billion yuan and accounted for about a quarter of real estate sales in Dalian, but space to expand in Dalian was limited. In order to become large-scale, Wanda decided on cross-regional development, and practice has proven that this step was quite right. If, at that time, we had not had the bravery to step out, then today's Wanda would not exist.

Around 2000 the Chinese residential real estate market was flourishing, and supply did not meet demand, but I think the residential real estate industrial model was flawed. First, residential real estate is a cyclical industry. Globally, when a country's urbanization rate reaches 70-80%, the residential real estate market will atrophy, and though trading volume remains, the vast majority is second-hand houses. Secondly, the cash flow of residential real estate is unstable. If items are sold there is a cash flow, but if items aren't sold the cash flow is cut off. In order for the business to maintain sustainable development and pursue long-term and stable cash flows, Wanda decided to transition to commercial real estate. Now we have been going at it for 14 years and have not yet come across any true nationwide competitors.

Each year Wanda Commercial Real Estate's start volume is more than ten million square meters, and completed openings are several million square meters. Moreover, the opening area has annual growth of the order of magnitude of a million square meters. Last year, 4.1 million square meters were opened; this year more than 5 million square meters; and next year more than 6 million square meters. But commercial real estate is still cyclical, and after China's urbanization is complete there will no longer be major growth. Now there are many commercial real estate imitators, and local overheating has emerged. The media has written articles saying that Wanda is entering cultural tourism and transnational development to dig a business "moat." To put it bluntly, it is to establish a new competitive advantage. For Wanda, cultural tourism, especially large-scale culture and tourism projects, means that it is more difficult to have imitators and competitors because the key factors in culture and tourism are not capital and land. The core is creativity, technology and talent.

3. The Branding Influence is Huge

Concerning the cultural industry, I once said that the vast majority of industries have ceilings, with the exception of the cultural industry, one which has no ceilings. Having no ceilings has two implications: first, the brand influence has no ceilings. A piece of work may have a very profound and long-lasting influence, even so much as to bring about a revolution in some respect. For example, the movie "*Avatar*," not only had a large branding influence, but also drove the promotion of IMAX movie technology. IMAX technology appeared in 1963, but because of the cost, film sources and a variety of other reasons, the promotion of IMAX never got off the ground. With the screening of "*Avatar*," everybody experienced particularly good IMAX 3D viewing effects, and that promoted the rapid growth of IMAX and changed the fate of this cinematic technology. Secondly, there is no profit ceiling. For Wanda Cinemas, for example, after-tax profit margins surpassed 10%, greatly exceeding what many people imagined. The Cinematic Technology Entertainment Project that Wanda is constructing in Wuhan has investments of 3.5 billion yuan, which is enormous. However, after the project opens it is expected to reach annual revenue of 1 billion yuan, an extremely impressive and long-duration profit.

II. The Content of Wanda Cultural Industry

Rather than merely setting about the content industry (which by the way still faces many restrictions), Wanda's Cultural Industry is innovating in terms of technology and form. In so doing it is achieving a large scale and it is avoiding risk. For example, shooting a film: due to content review and restrictions on other aspects, it is very difficult to achieve rapid growth. Performing arts are the same; a play must be better. Revenue of 20 million yuan is extraordinary, but it takes 100 plays before one is able to top one Wuhan Cinema Park. Wanda Cultural Industry has given prominence to amusement and entertainment businesses, made the chain, and created the scale effect. Wanda's Cultural Industry is involved in the following areas:

1. The Cultural Tourism City

The Cultural Tourism City is the epitome of Wanda Cultural Industry. Wanda Group, with many years of accumulating rich experience accumulated in business, culture, and the tourism industry, blazed new trails to form the world's first comprehensive, large-scale cultural tourism business project. It is the sole creation of its kind in the world, the design team is assembled of masters, and Wanda possesses the property rights to the three main characteristics. The total investment of each Wanda Culture and Tourism City exceeded 20 billion yuan, and includes a super-sized Wanda Plaza, a large outdoor theme park, a hotel group, a large stage show, a bar street and so on. Now Wanda Changbai Mountain International Resort has opened, two major cultural projects of Wuhan Central Cultural District will open in the fourth quarter, and then the project will be complete. Next year Xishuangbanna International Resort will open, and then there will be two or more cultural tourism projects opening annually. Wanda already has nine of the planned 12-15 cultural tourism cities that will spread across the nation: Wuhan, Changbai Mountain, Xishuangbanna, Harbin, Qingdao, Nanchang, Hefei, Wuxi, and Guilin.

2. Cinematic Industry

Wanda's film industry has a complete industry chain, including everything from a movie and television base, production, distribution, screening and a film festival, making it the only one in the world. Although Wanda Film Production Company had a late start, the results are good. It was established last year, and this year it released two movies. The investment in these two movies was very small and the profits substantial. "*Police Story 3*," which earned about 600 million yuan at the box office, had less than 100 million yuan invested in it, and "*Beijing Love Story*," which earned about 400 million yuan at the box office, had an investment of 30 million. In the latter half of this year, Wanda still plans to release three or four more movies.

Wanda Cinemas, adopting Hollywood's industrial model, shoots what a specialized decision-making team decides. Unlike many Chinese companies that rely on just one or two directors and one or two actors, Wanda does not sign directors and actors but takes the modern enterprise system of the film industry. With regards to film distribution, Wanda has a distribution company in America and has incorporated a distribution company in China. This distribution company will account for half of the shares of the Chinese film market, meaning from now on Wanda has a right to speak in the publishing field. Wanda has Wanda Cinemas in China, has acquired AMC in the United States Wanda, and is still looking for new acquisition opportunities in Europe and America. Currently, Wanda accounts for roughly 10% of global movie box office, and the goal is to reach 20% by 2020. In that year, global box offices are predicted to be worth approximately US$35-40 billion. If Wanda achieves its objective, it means that cinema revenues alone will reach US$7-8 billion. With total investment of nearly 50 billion yuan, Wanda is making the world's largest film and television industrial park, bidding for the Qingdao International Film Festival, and planning to create a Chinese cultural brand with global reach and appeal.

3. Performing Arts

Wanda's collection of performing arts contains stage shows, water shows, stage variations and high-tech integration, instead of traditional cinemas. Currently there are four projects under construction in Wuhan, Xishuangbanna, Qingdao and Wuxi. This year Wuhan's "*Han Show*" will open, and will take the world's performing arts to new heights.

4. Film Technology Entertainment

Wanda film technology entertainment is a collection of the world's leading film technology and entertainment projects. Currently there are six projects under construction in Wuhan, Harbin, Nanchang, Hefei, Wuxi and Guilin. Wuhan Film Technology Park opens this year, and is the world's only comprehensive film technology entertainment project. Using 3D film technology and a dynamic platform, people can be integrated into movie scenes and interactive games.

5. Theme Parks

The theme parks constructed by Wanda are world-class. Currently there are six projects under construction in Xishuangbanna, Harbin, Qingdao, Nanchang, Hefei and Guilin, of which both Xishuangbanna and Nanchang will be opened in 2015. Shanghai Disneyland is also currently being built, and while a single Wanda theme park is not necessarily better than Disney, "one good tiger is no match for a pack of wolves." Wanda is building up more than a dozen theme parks in China, which will greatly reduce Disney's market share in China.

6. Children's Entertainment Chain

Wanda spent three to four years to research and develop the children entertainment chain's completely new format, which relies mainly on children experiencing interactive content for play. It combines children's education, retail, food and so on. Wanda Children's Entertainment Chain is divided into two levels, a small area of roughly 5,000 square meters called "Baby King," of which 11 projects will be opened this year and a large area around of 20,000 square meters called "Kids Park." They are the first in the world, and it is believed that they will cause quite a stir when they hit the market.

Wanda commissioned and bought the intellectual property rights from the world's five most famous companies who researched and developed 86 different products for children's amusement. For example, children can experience the role of a fire fighter, from receiving the fire report to simulating a fire fighter driving to fight the fire. On the way there, there will be 3D simulation of fire effects. To prevent spraying people, the spray guns have a fixed orientation toward the simulated ignition point to put out the fire. The children's education does not use traditional school education content, and is mainly made up of activities like dancing, playing the drums, ice skating, singing and so on.

7. Wholesale KTV Chain

There are currently 81 KTVs open, and this year 24 more will open. It is the largest-scale KTV operation globally.

8. Others

Wanda manages investments in the magazines "*China Times*," a financial weekly, and "*Popular Cinema*." Wanda is dedicated to collecting top quality paintings and calligraphy from contemporary Chinese artists, and has amassed a collection of 100 great masters and 1,000 museum collection-level artworks.

III. Characteristics of Wanda Cultural Industry

1. A Combination of Diverse Factors

Wanda's Cultural Industry will not simply compartmentalize with culture studying culture and tourism studying tourism. Wanda hits with the combination punches: the greater the combination of factors, the larger the scale, the stronger the power. Wanda cultural tourism project integrates technological, cultural, touristic, and commercial features to form a comprehensive cultural travel business, such as Wuhan Central Cultural District, which is the first Chinese city with a program called Central Cultural District. Inside ten cultural projects are set up, including the world's first Film Technology Park and the *Han Show*, two significant cultural projects. The Chu River, which connects Sha Lake to East Lake, runs through the center of Wuhan Cultural District. Han Street, a commercial pedestrian street, runs along the river. Han Street Central has the Han Street Wanda Plaza, a five-star and a premier hotel, and more than one million square meters of offices and one million square meters of housing. Changbaishan International Resort is Wanda's first cultural tourism project to open. It boasts Asia's largest skiing area, totaling 43 slopes with a combined length of tens of kilometers. There are three world-class golf courses, nine hotels with more than 5,000 beds, and a 900 meter long commercial pedestrian street with more than 100 businesses, restaurants, bars, cinemas, karaoke, stage performances, spas and anything else one could think of.

2. High Technological Content

Wanda Cultural Industry's most prominent distinctive feature is its high technological content. For example, in Qingdao Wanda put on the "*Ultimate Car Show*," which is a completely innovative and high-tech project. This project has been under research and development for many years and is having its global premiere in the first half of 2017.

The *Ultimate Car Show* and the *Han Show* are very different; the *Han Show* focuses on cultural tastes, and the *Ultimate Car Show* provokes a thrill. The show has a circular track and a multitude of electric vehicles doing stunts at 120 kilometers per hour and above. The combination with the performing arts is breathtaking. Wanda's shows chal- lenge the human body to the extreme, so performers are hard to cultivate, and their performance life cycle is short. Once beyond a certain age, they can no longer perform. Wanda places a lot of consideration on technological equipment; the *Han Show* has dozens of devices, there are 14 sets of equipment just for underwater. The high-tech content makes for even more dazzling effects.

3. The Integration of Global Resources

The cultural industry is a creative industry; the most important things are creativity and talent. Only by integrating global resources can world-class innovation be achieved. Take the *Han Show*, for example. The construction and stage equipment were ideas from the world's top architectural and art design master, Mr. Mark Fisher, who was the artistic director for the opening and closing ceremonies of the Beijing Olympics, the Guangzhou Asian Games and the London Olympics.The program is by creative director Mr. Franco Dragone, one of the world's best stage artists and a renowned master. He directed Las Vegas' "*O*" and "*La Rêve*" as well as Macau's "*The House of Dancing Water*." Wanda Cultural Tourism Planning and Research Institute has over 300 people, half of whom are foreign, and many of whom are top global players in their industries. In particular the theme park Chief Packaging Officer, the Chief Theatre Designer, the Chief of Film Special Effects and six other chiefs are among the biggest industry names in the world. This kind of top talent is difficult to cultivate alone, so Wanda relies on high salaries to lure them in. If they are really unwilling to join the company, Wanda signs exclusive cooperation agreements with their companies or buys their intellectual property rights.

4. Prominent Chinese Elements

Wanda has made cultural tourism an important development direction for the future, as the main industry must reflect Chinese culture and cannot rely on photocopying foreign things. Take the *Han Show* for example: the architecture is modeled after a traditional Chinese red lantern; the program is called the *Han Show*, "Han" referring to the Chinese Han ethnicity, or going further referring to the ancient Chinese legend of Chu and Han, or even referring to the city of Wuhan; the story is also a Chinese story. Wanda hopes to create many theme parks throughout the country, and each place's theme park designer will integrate local cultural characteristics. If all parks follow the same pattern, then people will not want to travel to Wanda's parks in other locations. For instance, Xishuangbanna's park areas are designed as a tropical rain forest, an ancient tea route, a butterfly kingdom, an aquatic park and more, all of which reflect rich characteristics ingrained in the local culture. Wanda also requires that all theme parks have several large one-of-a-kind rides. To do so, Wanda and the world's two best theme park equipment-manufacturing companies have reached an agreement, in which important equipment can be customized while Wanda possesses the intellectual property rights to ensure that others cannot imitate.

The advantages of Wanda Cultural Project's prominent Chinese elements, reflection of local characteristics, and exclusive customized equipment will gradually become apparent in future operations. When the Wuxi Wanda City Project began, Wanda "declared war" with Shanghai Disney. We have surpassed Shanghai Disney on two core indexes with a grasp on park visits and operating revenue. This is due to Disney having only one theme park and not having changed the model in decades. Not only does Wuxi Wanda City have an outdoor theme park, but it also has an enormous indoor Wanda Plaza. Inside there are numerous rides as well as large stage shows, hotels, bars, etc. Altogether, these are more attractive, leading to more park visits and naturally rising revenues. Wuxi Wanda City is located at the heart of the Yangtze River Delta, an excellent location.

Furthermore, Wanda has national marketing capabilities through the acquisition of nationwide travel agencies. Through the establishment and perfection of the tourism industry chain, in the future a large number of tourists can be transported for the Wanda Cultural Tourism Project.

5. Independent Intellectual Property Rights

Wanda's Cultural Industry Project emphasizes independent creation and manufacturing. If Wanda cannot do it themselves, they will need to commission the design and buy out the intellectual property rights. Once in America, I saw a program combining the live actions of a real person with 3-D. The collaboration was between a software company and Disney and used a split method, but Wanda cannot accept this style. In the cultural industry Wanda develops like a chain, and discussing cooperation divisions one by one is not only troublesome but also makes us vulnerable to the control of others. For the purpose of scale development, Wanda would rather spend more money and obtain the independent intellectual property rights. To buy the intellectual property rights of the Qingdao *Ultimate Car Show* Wanda spent US$10 million.

When Mr. Fisher just began coming up with ideas for the *Han Show's* moving light-emitting diode (LED) lights, many people said they couldn't be done, but we didn't give up. At last, with the support of the Mechanical Institution of the People's Liberation Army (PLA) General Armament Department and after numerous modifications and tests we finally succeeded. Now the equipment is installed. Each weighs 200 tons and has the freedom of movement to shift angles and directions. This enables infinite variety for the stage background and gives the program director more room for creativity.

IV. The Prospects for Wanda Cultural Industry

1. The Profits of Opened Industry

What is industry? Industry is operating according to market mechanisms and one's own ability to form cyclic production capacity. Industry is definitely not relying on government subsidies to maintain existence. In the cultural industry, Wanda's most basic requirement is that it is profitable; it will never be keeping up appearances. All of the cultural industry projects that Wanda has already opened are profitable, and the profitability is satisfactory. In 2012 Wanda took over the world's second-largest cinema chain, AMC, American Movie Company.

Pre-purchase, AMC had suffered losses for several years, but after Wanda took over they achieved profitability. Then, last December on the New York Stock Exchange, the listing was successful. Wanda's acquisition of AMC was an actual investment of roughly US$700 million, plus we assumed AMC's debt of US$1.9 billion. Last year, not only did the listing raise US400 million in cash, but the market value of the AMC stock held by Wanda was also twice the value of the original investment, and recently stocks were up nearly three times.

Why wasn't AMC profitable under American operation for so many years, but when Wanda took over it became profitable? The key factor is that before Wanda took over there was no real owner, just five shareholders acting as funds and only thinking about how to sell the company for a good price. AMC's CEO told me that within one year he received more than 100 buyers. Under such circumstances, how could the management team operate carefully? Wanda's acquisition of AMC is the opposite. First, they spoke with the core management level. After Wanda's acquisition they signed a five-year work contract, established an incentive mechanism, and came up with a shared profits reward for management. Only after all of these were negotiated did Wanda talk with shareholders about buying the company. This move awakened the initiative of the management level, and AMC quickly reversed losses and achieved profitability. Meanwhile, Wanda adopted control measures to monitor in real-time each individual AMC cinema's daily income and costs. In the end, there were no obstacles to our targets.

2. Good Expectations for Unopened Projects

On June 20 of this year, Wuhan's *Han Show* and Movie Technology Park, two projects that represent the future direction of Wanda Cultural Industry, will transfer operations, begin worldwide ticket sales, and officially premiere in December. We expect that show tickets within the first six months will be sold out in a flash. In other words, customers that hear that the story in the *Han Show* is good and want to go see the performance will have to buy tickets six months in advance. Wuxi Wanda City, on opening, is expected to have an annual flow of around 20 million people and an annual income of three to five billion yuan, certainly more than Shanghai Disney. Through practice, Wanda wants to tell Chinese people that American companies are not necessarily stronger than Chinese ones.

3. Become a World-Class Cultural Enterprise

Each year, the world famous strategy consultant Roland Berger releases the "Top 50 Global Culture Industry Players Study." In 2012 Wanda ranked 38, and in 2013 the ranking is likely to be even closer to the top. Wanda's 2016 objective for the Cultural Industry is to push revenue to 40 billion yuan and enter into the world's top 20; Wanda's 2020 objective is to raise revenue to 80 billion yuan and enter into the world's top ten. Looking at the current implementation, Wanda will certainly achieve the goal ahead of schedule and become a world-class cultural enterprise.

Thank you everyone.

Q & A

Q: I have two questions. You just introduced so many Wanda Cultural Tourism Property Projects. First, what will be the on-going operational management practices with so many projects beginning construction each year? Second, when developing the cultural industry, what is Wanda's thinking with regards to the mobile Internet? Is there a specific strategy?

Wang Jianlin: Actually, no matter how well it is designed and how well it is built, the final key is operations. This is the only key to whether or not you can earn money. I often say, of course the level of technique is important, but the key is the path, and what is the path? Do not assume it is a strategy or an innovation. Wrong, it is people. From my own experience and from Wanda's development, I deeply appreciate that. People are the money and the cause, so talent is decisive. We just spoke about cultural tourism having hundreds of innovators with a number of foreigners. These are not Wanda employees but Wanda's cooperative partners and cannot become fixed cooperative partners. In that case, I buy out the intellectual property rights and commission the development. Usually when the project starts, we establish a completely international operations team. The Chinese talent for projects such as Wuhan's *Han Show* and Film Technology Park is still scarce. The CEOs are all hired abroad. Take theme parks: for example, our theme park management team requested the Vice President of Disney International, and the theme park department requested the Chairman of Hong Kong Disney. We are also in talent development; the Wanda Institute in the China Institute of Business is definitely number one. We ask those teachers to attend class. However, talent development is slow, and what is there to do when it is too late? Dig, headhunt, and dig. I now have cooperation with more than 50 headhunting companies, close to 20 of which are international. Take Qingdao Oriental Movie Metropolis for example, the project has now just begun, but Qingdao Industrial Park's CEO candidates will soon be put into position. The opening is only in 2017, so why position them this early? The CEO, COO, and CTO will all be placed first; I am not afraid of spending on these management costs because after spending time with the design team and the construction team, they will have a grasp on many things. For my film festival we also found a globally known CEO; this person will probably be put into position in May. The film festival will only be set up in 2016 or 2017, but they will still be put into position just as early. For each position we require a Chinese and foreign pair-up; if the CEO is a foreigner, then there will certainly be a Chinese person (or at least an ethnic Chinese) as Executive VP. Currently we are blazing trails for many new projects. Depending on our own training alone is really quite slow, so if you go to Wanda you will see that it is very international. In the elevators there are often foreigners, but we have one condition. Generally, those able to speak Chinese have priority in recruitment. I push for employees to speak Chinese because of circumstances. For instance, if a foreign employee went to a meeting with me but the boss did not speak English, I would not be able to anticipate what would happen. If, worldwide, there were ten thousand Chinese companies like Wanda, the promotion of the Chinese language would be much easier.

Second, It is now the age of the Internet. Although Ma Yun and I have a bet, it is just a joke, and although it is a joke, it actually represents two types of thought and two ways of thinking about how to view the Internet. I had to represent traditional industry, but in reality I am not engaged in retail. Therefore, I can tell him the Internet is good, but who will talk about bricks-and-mortar commerce?

Within Wanda, I already require that all companies develop on the Internet, and must have an Internet line of thought. Wanda's own O2O (online-to-offline) e-commerce company has already done online tests in six plazas. At the end of this year, this will be extended to 110 Wanda Plazas and all hotels. Our e-commerce has most of its own features. If the Internet is not combined with offline, the "O" is not complete. The Internet is just the upper half of the circle. My point of view is that in ten years there will be no pure bricks-and-mortar enterprises, nor will there be pure Internet companies, but there will certainly be a combination of online and offline. As for the Internet, how does one ultimately move in that direction? It is surely through integration. Do not assume that e-commerce companies only engage in e-commerce; they can also engage in culture and videos, why? Because it is a developmental necessity, if one does not engage in the Internet it probably becomes more terrifying. This is unlike us. A new subversive technology appears, and this business could instantaneously go from being a 100 billion yuan business to 10 billion. The Internet industry is also not like real industry. In real industry if the cash flow is good, the method advances. With a long-term, stable cash flow, it's possible that valuation is not too high and development speed is not fast, but the thinking is also not very fast. I believe the ultimate development trend is integration; there is no single completely distinctive Internet company. That is my opinion.

Q: I have three questions about the *Han Show*. First, approximately how many spectator seats are in the Red Lantern? Second, how much will tickets cost? Third, the use of water is important in this performance. I know that for a long period of time the temperature is quite high for the Las Vegas water shows and Macau's *"The House of Dancing Water."* Yet, Wuhan has a very long winter, which poses the problem of water temperatures. I believe the water temperature can be resolved, but this will increase costs. Also, the water in winter performances may bring mist. I would like to know, have you considered these issues?

Wang Jianlin: I was involved in the research and development for the *Han Show* and participated in probably more than 50 meetings. Now, my main focus at Wanda Group is to participate creatively. First, there are a little more than 2,000 seats and 140 VIP seats. There are approximately 400-450 performances annually. There are no performances on Mondays, and there is one added show on both Saturdays and Sundays. As for the tickets, in the initial six months of the show – the period for which we are basically sold out – all tickets are 500 yuan. A ticket price of 1,000 yuan could support our current investment, so after six months there may be a price increase. However, we will also consider China's actual situation. We can calculate: if there are 400 performances per year, that is approximately more than 100 million people, with tickets priced at 1,000 yuan, it is more than one billion yuan in revenue.

And for the third question, how will we deal with water temperature and fog? The team's building and machinery and equipment creator is Mr. Mark Fisher who is also the designer of *"O," "La Rêve"* and Macau's *"House of Dancing Water."* The artistic director, Mr. Dragone, is also the founder of worldwide water shows, of which there are only three; the two in Las Vegas and the one in Macau, so I'm sure this issue has been considered.

Q: You put a great emphasis on technology, but would not like to enter into content. However, in this era, content is king. Have you heard of (the Korean television show) *"My Love from the Star"*?

Wang Jianlin: I know of it, but I haven't seen it.

Q: But *My Love from the Star* has already had a profound impact on our youth, especially young women. How do you view this issue? Here you are talking about Wanda being international as a core concept, a one hundred-year enterprise. Apart from responsibility for themselves and shareholders, what more are you hoping to bring to our enterprises? Will there be content development, will content be improved to impact Europe and America and spread Chinese culture?

Wang Jianlin: It is impossible to not value the content, I am saying, "We shouldn't compare content and innovation, and don't place the content first." What is the *Han Show*? Solely form? It is content. You wouldn't say that theme parks are just roller coasters, right? Of course there is content, for instance Xishuangbanna's several themes: the Ancient Tea Route, Butterfly Kingdom and the Rainforest. This in itself is content; it has a position, and every place is different, such as Heilongjiang's Snow Village. I don't think that the content you are talking about is the content of the cultural industry, merely the content of movies and television series. The saying "content is king" is not entirely correct. There is another saying you should not forget, "means are king," and some people even say, "marketing is king." I often visit Hollywood's big television companies and movie companies. The basic investment is "442." 40 percent is production costs, 40 percent for marketing and 20 percent is the cost of an actor. This point I thought was very strange and asked why would 20 percent of the total be for actors? I got the answer that it was a golden rule, and if the money the actor wanted exceeded 20 percent of the costs, they would find a different actor. This is the Hollywood industrial model with fixed costs. If you want more I won't give it to you and will switch for a different person. China still hasn't adopted the Hollywood industrial model, and the current model is flawed; 70-80 percent of the costs are taken by the actors, which definitely can't result in good production. China still isn't into the real film industrial era but is in the era of small workshops and self-employed films. Companies rely on hiring one or two directors and signing one or two well-known actors. Once our film industry develops to US$10 or US$20 billion, it will inevitably change. I'll give an example; *Beijing Love Story* cost 30 million yuan. It did 400 million yuan at the box office, due in large part to marketing. Of course, when compared, content is certainly arranged first, but it cannot be said so simply. The reason we don't stress the content is because we want to take in more and do it bigger.

Another is our corporate philosophy, International Wanda, a centennial enterprise. The company's slogan can't be too long. If we put all this social responsibility and love for the workers into it, then it would become too long and nobody would remember. For 27 years, Wanda corporate culture's core philosophy was eight characters long and has been updated three times. When I did business in 1988, in that time for business it was "you cheat me" and "I cheat you." There was no way to know what to do, no contracts, no property titles, and no licenses. I think those days were very strange, so back then I proposed seven words for corporate culture, "conduct oneself honestly and handle matters astutely." There is a well-known European proverb saying: Fool me once shame on you, fool me twice shame on me. Right? Handle matters astutely. A few years later, in 1998, the corporation earned some money and crossed regions. When I felt like I had a little money, I thought I should have a feeling of social responsibility, so at that time our corporate culture was updated to "creating wealth together, sharing with society." In 2002, our corporation had our third cultural upgrade. I thought our horizons should internationalize, as the final objective is an international corporation, International Wanda, so we gave ourselves objective targets. By 2020 we must be in the World's Top 100, have revenue of US$100 billion, and become a multinational corporation, for the nation but also to make ourselves proud. Again, it is a centennial enterprise and hopes for a little longevity. So you said there is no social responsibility; that is only the literal understanding. You also talked about the impact on Europe and America, does there need to be a cultural impact on Europe and America? Yes of course, but I think at the present stage we need to advance the cultural impact on China. Once I have managed this with Chinese people, then let's speak again about doing it with foreigners.

Q: First, will AMC cinemas meet our expectations? Second, the homogeneity in domestic commercial cinemas is quite serious. Wanda Cinema has tried to bring forth many new ideas, including *"I am a Singer"* and *"The Voice of China."* What are the operation's future plans?

Wang Jianlin: First the question regarding AMC, since Chinese people bought it, it will surely have some effect. We operate with our original team and original model, yet with much interference, in particular last December when we were already listed on the market. We still must follow market rules. However, as a major shareholder, we can still raise requirements. For example, I require them to screen at least five Chinese films annually. I'll give you some data: in 2012 we merged with AMC, and in that year we released eight Chinese films. In 2013, we released 13 Chinese films. This created a history of China in the United States. One year before this, just screening one Chinese movie was not bad, and that basically was not market-oriented – say, the state invested money to contract several cinemas to screen one movie twice, and at once it was returned. In past development of our cultural projects, comrade Li Changchun did a report for me and said four very vivid things: "Finance is the investment source, leadership is basically the audience, prize-winning is the main objective, and the warehouse is the final destination." He said that the development of culture depends on industry, and central leadership awareness is a basis for our future development. We are entirely market-oriented; many films go out, and good ones may get more than US$10 million in the box office, like *The Grandmaster*. Inferior films may beunable to get even US$100,000 at the box office. And why don't Chinese movies have good results? First, they aren't English films; when Chinese people watch foreign films with subtitles it is good enough, we even do English subtitles. However, Americans did not respond as fast and said it is not OK. They were unwilling to spend on the production costs and asked how there could be good profits. For the future of Chinese film to be truly global there has to be English thinking, and films shot in English. Another is the need to market. We say the film is good, and we release it in the U.S. However, there is simply no thought of earning money or marketing in the U.S. No actor is even sent there. You just sell as many as you can. We may also have this attitude, so the results are not that great. But I believe this can change, and it is just a matter of time.

The second thing you talked about was Chinese film market innovation. Last year the box office of the Chinese film industry was just over 20 billion yuan. The box office of the world's two largest markets (Europe and America) both surpassed US$10 billion. The worldwide box office was a little more than US$30 billion. In these developed markets, it is not possible that all cinemas release the same movie. Only China has this kind of special phenomenon; the whole country's cinemas all release the same movie, and the discharge rate is high. This is an indication that the market is not developed. In developed markets, many cinemas buy the broadcasting rights or a few together, franchised or divided, etc. Therefore, apart from a few very large films that are US$200-300 million in production, it almost can't be said that there is a unified film release. Wanda is also doing some innovation. According to my judgment, in 2018 our film market shares may pass those of the U.S., and surpass US$10 billion. So long as the scale of the market gets to that degree, leading cinemas, for example ours, can at that time set off from the viewpoint of supporting certain content and supporting the best directors, not excluding screenings of certain content that we customize or support.

Chapter Seven

O2O

Creating Smart Shopping Malls

29 August, 2014 – Speech from the Strategic Cooperation Agreement Signing Ceremony for Wanda E-Commerce

First, on behalf of my one hundred thousand colleagues I would like to give a warm welcome and many thanks to chairman Robin Li and chairman Pony Ma, the leaders of Baidu and Tencent, and all of our friends from the media for your presence at today's signing ceremony, and offer my congratulations on the establishment of Wanda E-Commerce.

When we were just chatting in the lounge, chairman Pony Ma mentioned that the "Commerce" in "E-Commerce" is not appropriate for the company I aim to establish. Internally we originally thought of calling it Electronic Information Technology Company, but didn't think it was well thought out, so we temporarily called it E-Commerce. However, this name probably led you all to mistakenly think E-Commerce is going to sell merchandise, so we still need to mull over the name.

Today I will cover four points: Number one, O2O is the largest piece of the e-commerce pie. Regardless of whether worldwide or in China, e-commerce has developed for so many years, and all kinds of large e-commerce business platforms have been built up. However, there still is no O2O integration platform. The total of China's consumer market is expected to be around 30 trillion yuan this year, of which roughly little more than one third goes in a shopping bag. A part of what belongs in a shopping bag can be bought online: essentially books, cosmetics and clothing – the latter taking up the biggest chunk. But nearly two thirds can neither be carried in a bag, nor be sold online. This is the larger market: the consumption of experiences – watching movies, dining out, entertainment, etc. I have yet to see a platform able to turn this into a smart consumer market – a platform achieving the integration between online and offline. Because of this, the three of us have spoken about the need to create such an e-commerce platform. This will be the biggest piece of the e-commerce pie. With the rise in purchasing power, more and more experiences will be consumed, rather than purchased as tradable goods. This is true everywhere you look around the world. O2O may well become the biggest piece of the e-commerce market pie, but this pie has not yet been sliced. Such a platform has not yet emerged.

Number two, the opportunities are equal. O2O has only just begun. Numerous online platforms are considering how to infiltrate the offline market. Some offline companies, like Wanda, are looking for ways to go online and to integrate. As all have just begun, there is no genuine O2O platform with platform technologies. Under these circumstances, I think the opportunities will be equal for everyone. Since there is not yet a major platform, we are willing to exert efforts in this regard.

Number three, there must be a genuine Internet Line of Thought. What do I mean by this? Currently almost all the companies that claim to be O2O are online, so there seems to be a consensus – as though only online companies can do O2O. In reality, I don't think this is an Internet Line of Thought. An Internet Line of Thought is innovative and has no set formula. Some people have questioned how Wanda could do e-commerce as it normally does real estate. Today our company is being established at a formal signing ceremony, but we have actually been building the team for more than six months. Many of my colleagues asked me whether we are going from online-to-offline or from offline-to-online. I told them both of these ideas are wrong; we should not have a fixed notion of online and offline. We want to integrate online and offline and form an interactive, integrated consumption model. Wanda E-Commerce will certainly not sell merchandise, but will sell services and make good use of its offline terminals. China's current shopping malls have been developing for decades and its bazaars for a century. There are plenty of parking lots, but currently no smart parking technology is even connected to the parking lots. When customers come, they don't know if there is a parking space or not. Some people complain that from the entrance it takes two hours until they are even able to go down. Once inside, they do not know where the parking space is as every floor has over 1,000 parking spaces, so they waste a lot of time driving around in circles looking for a parking space. After they have finished their shopping and leave the mall, they have forgotten where in the parking lot they have parked and amble around one or two floors of the parking lot in vain. With O2O and an intelligent positioning application, finding the car has become a piece of cake.

My thinking is very much in line with that of Pony and Robin. We are establishing this company out of a desire to research how to make the offline mall, etc. smart. This is O2O, not selling things. As for when the physical image of e-commerce will emerge, I think it may be next year. Some people say that Wanda E-Commerce has already been established for two years, but this is actually not true. Our own data center, our own smart systems, our software... none of it has been fully developed. The soft launch is at the end of this year, and it will officially go online at the end of next year. Measured from the end of this year, maybe in two or three years' time – or possibly a little sooner, in one or two years – it will become clear what kind of company Wanda E-Commerce is and what kind of value it generates.

Number four, being in e-commerce is both a need and a responsibility. This is not just bragging. The worldwide consumer market is tens of trillions of US dollars and by 2020, China's consumer market alone will certainly surpass US$10 trillion. This year it has already surpassed 30 trillion yuan. Still, no O2O platform has emerged so far for such a large consumer market. Our O2O company has announced plans to invest five billion yuan, the first investment in which all three of us have participated in. In reality, over the last five years we have invested a total of close to 20 billion yuan. Also, we may introduce strategic investors.

For an O2O experiment, the amount of money is certainly enormous. So many colleagues in the industry have told us they will wait until we have done e-commerce, because they cannot afford to do it and it is too much effort. They want to see whether we can do it. If one day our experiment is a success, there will be five billion users in 2020, excluding Wanda itself. And there is the possibility of transforming into an open platform accessible to all Chinese resorts, cinema, culture and dining. This would have tremendous value. We are doing all the exploration for the sake of the entire offline industry. I want to again thank chairmans Robin Li and Pony Ma for attending the signing ceremony and express my gratitude for Baidu, Tencent and Wanda reaching a cooperation agreement. Thank you everyone.

Appendix 1

Chairman and CEO of Baidu Robin Li: Leader of Online and Offline Convergence

Dear Chairman Wang Jianlin and Chairman Pony Ma, I am truly happy to be able to attend the Wanda E-Commerce Cooperation Agreement Signing Ceremony. I think this cooperation is representative of a trend, a trend that chairman Jianlin just spoke about; it is a trend of integration. It is not going from one direction to the other; it isn't about moving from online to offline or offline to online. In fact, I often say the same internally, that both sides should meet in the middle. Bridges start from both sides and rise together in the middle, and this is the best way. The integration of online and offline is such a way as well, moreover I firmly believe that this way is representative of a trend, representative of the trend of future development and representative of the trend of the development of the mobile Internet.

In Baidu's operating history of over ten years in China, we have been continuously been trying to persuade businesses in the real economy to go online. To date there may be hundreds of thousands of businesses that have acquired new customers and business through the Baidu platform. The entire IT industry is changing rapidly, and technology is progressing quickly. Our real economy is embracing the new technologies and changes, but the pace is not that fast. Since last year I've been anxious, and at the 2015 Baidu Union Summit I spoke about the accelerated elimination of traditional industries by the Internet. If they do not embrace the Internet, new technologies and the mobile Internet their elimination may be complete.

After so many years in this industry, we have gotten the perception that the businesses accepting new technologies are not large businesses, not mature businesses, but rather small businesses. Baidu's earliest customers were online fresh flower stores, and they were the first to accept new technology. It will mark quite a change, the day that large businesses too are ready to fully embrace the possibilities brought about by Internet technology. About six months ago, chairman Jianlin and I both realized that such opportunities are pretty good for us. On one hand, China's Internet has gone through many years of development, has six or seven hundred million Netizens, and the mobile Internet is growing even faster. While we used to think that Internet technologies and innovations came primarily from the United States, nowadays a lot of new technologies and new commerce models are sprouting in China. Many innovations are originating in China too.

A few years ago I went to America and spoke with famous industry founders and CEOs. They kept on asking: "What does China have? Isn't China just copying American things?" Now, I'll go talk to them, and they'll say, "China has a lot of innovations; we should pay close attention to China." I told my American friend that I have a house in America, and he replied, "And I want to buy a house in China to visit often and see the country." A group of American businessmen and entrepreneurs have been coming regularly to China of late, not to figure out how to get their products into China, but to see what innovations are made in China every day. This is a truly encouraging sign. We live in a very encouraging era. Sometimes I say that we live in a magical era: China's market is tremendously attractive and is growing fast. Technological innovation and progress are faster than ever. The innovations in a single year are equivalent to the innovations that used to take a decade or more. The continuous development of artificial intelligence, in particular, has brought us many opportunities, including O2O opportunities. If someone is shopping at Wanda and sees a beautiful skirt, they can take a picture, and you know it is sold at Wanda. You may see a poster and know that Wanda Cinemas has several screenings of this specific movie, so you can complete seat selection and payment. The combination of online and offline has already moved away from the era of the PC. The PC era, using Baidu as a representative search engine, has been about connecting people and information. As people enter keywords on the keyboard, we help them find the information they want. In the mobile Internet era, what we do more of is connecting people with services. When you have a demand, not only can we tell you where it can be satisfied, but we can also immediately satisfy your demand. Take movie tickets, for example. I want to watch a movie, and I can choose a seat online, walk in and watch the movie. I think this is a trend that has only just begun.

Such a trend requires that Internet companies and the real economy have tighter integration. Wanda, Tencent and Baidu are able to effectively advance the connection of people and services and to better advance the rapid and healthy growth of the entire economy. Often we see that offline businesses don't have sufficiently effective business models. Take plane tickets for instance. Aircraft are never full. If they could be filled to capacity, the operating costs would be lower. It is the same principle not only for plane tickets but for cinemas, restaurants and karaoke bars. I think how we use technology, operational means and a combined mode of online and offline to enhance the operating results of all levels of the economy is a challenge. But, even more than that, it is an opportunity for us. I hope that through the announcement of Wanda E-Commerce and with the cooperation among three companies, we can witness the creation of new standards for many companies over many, many years, so that the integration between online and offline is done flawlessly. I hope that Wanda E-Commerce continues to create new glories with each passing day. Thank you!

Tencent Chairman of the Board of Directors and CEO Pony Ma: Connecting Cooperation Partners to Transform Open Platforms

Good morning dear Chairman Jianlin and Chairman Robin, all colleagues of Wanda and Baidu!

I am honored to be able to attend today's Wanda E-Commerce launch ceremony. The name still doesn't seem to fit perfectly. I think the word may create a lot of misunderstanding for friends of the industry – with questions about whether or not we are three "local tycoons" getting together, redeveloping the field of e-commerce (which has already been developed for more than ten years) and initiating an attack. This would be a mistake, because it fails to clearly see the nature of the trend. Both chairmen just raised a number of points that were mentioned when we were chatting before the meeting. The word 'e-commerce' is not entirely accurate.

After reflecting for a moment, I thought that the difference lies in how we use the Internet and the mobile Internet technology to turn the immense undeveloped offline economic entity into smart commerce. I think this is putting it a bit more accurately.

Here is an enormous market, but it is complex, and it would be absolutely impossible to create using the line of thought and the abilities of a pure internet company. Mobile Internet and the Internet used to see the Internet as overturning, replacing and updating traditional businesses, but I feel that this is only the preliminary stage. In the future, the internet will allow many industries to move to a higher level. If a company refuses to use internet technology, it may fall behind its industry peers and be eliminated. There is nothing mysterious about the internet. It can be understood, just as electricity could be understood. Before there was electricity, banking and stock brokers developed, insurance and a great many industries thrived. Once electric power arrived, could the power companies destroy all other industries? Impossible! Could energy companies achieve a complete monopoly? Also impossible. All sectors in all industries have used new technologies and new capabilities to elevate their industry. There are plenty of opportunities. Of those that can seize opportunities in this wave, their competitiveness in the vertical market will far exceed unresponsive and slow-to-act companies.

Based on such a premise, we greatly respect every major player in the traditional industries. Deep industry support is not something that pure internet companies can do alone. Over the last six months to a year, much of the developmental thinking at Tencent has changed significantly. We have let go of many areas where we used to have no chance of using our own technology, our own capabilities and where we had to rely on cooperation with partners in the vertical market. We focus our energy on doing what we are best at: communications, social networking, and entertainment industries. Also using our core platform technologies, Tencent hopes to become a connector not only between people, but equally between people and services and a connector between people and businesses. We are not demanding to be in charge. We just need to contribute our value as a connector. We want to connect with other end connectors as partners and business organizations; this is why we have today's cooperation.

Over the past year or two, I've been in contact with Chairman Wang Jianlin several times. Robin and I paid a visit to Wanda, and Chairman Wang Jianlin introduced several cases, which were indeed eye-opening. In the past we thought that Wanda was just real estate, but actually after real estate Wanda developed many offline cultural industries and expanded in many areas, all of which were big eye-openers for us. Both Wang Jianlin and I say there are a lot of opportunities here in the entertainment field, online and offline, we happen to be doing the maximum with billions of yuan in sales. At present, online entertainment and offline entertainment are completely separate, and we feel that the future holds great business opportunities. These can't be completed through the computer or mobile phones but must be experienced offline. Through this example, one can see the multitude of collaboration opportunities.

When WeChat proposed the slogan "Connecting all," I actively promoted it. Using the mobile Internet has allowed many services to become more intelligent, and we see that all sectors are included, not only retail or only cultural. A lot of finance, telecommunications and other industries are involved. They all have so many O2O opportunities.

Today we take the first step to discovering how Baidu and Tencent can participate in Wanda's tremendous O2O integration. Through Internet technologies, people will be able to make people's lives more convenient, more intelligent, more efficient, more creative, and cooler. I think this is a highly beneficial attempt.

Abroad there is likewise no clear case that can serve as a reference. China's Internet is still developing. Many people used to ask how we could do it if it didn't exist abroad. But it has become clear that China's business models and many other aspects can lead the world. Take our own core communication; we see WeChat and QQ both use mobile Internet methods to blaze entirely new trails. As a lot of innovations in China do not have their match abroad, China has the ability to apply its own characteristics. As long as you are able to grasp what users need and what users feel is important, then business opportunities will exist. With this platform, I strongly support what Chairman Jianlin spoke about – that this is not just for Wanda. The released platform can be transformed into an open platform. On this basis, each vertical market, including the just-mentioned smart parking lot, smart tours and cultural industries' programm, can develop a brand new set of smart systems, fully open to all competitors and partners, to be further integrated.

You've seen today's cooperation. We all spoke of BAT (Baidu, Alibaba and Tencent). Rarely have we had major cooperation with Baidu. This time, for the first time, we go hand in hand. Many Internet businesses have clearly understood that the trend is towards integration with competitors. I am taking this opportunity to issue a message to the industry: you shouldn't consider competition among Internet companies as a cloud of smoke filling the air or a game of life and death. Actually, everyone has their own advantages and their own shortcomings; we should work together hand in hand to do something more. As long as the demands of the customers are met, we should attempt more cooperation.

I am last; thanks all media friends in attendance. Our prior press release was already written, and the outside world had some misunderstandings. We did not arrange a special question and answer session, and today we did not read manuscripts. We hope that we have answered all of your questions, thank you everyone.

Chapter Eight

Responsibility

Promoting Philanthropy in our Corporate Culture

16 August, 2014 – Statement at the First China Charity Forum

Good morning, dear guests!

The Wanda Group was established in 1988 and has been in existence for more than 27 years. As of June 30 of this year, we have donated more than 3.7 billion yuan in cash. In terms of nationwide corporations, this is the largest amount ever donated. China Charity has issued a total of eight awards, seven of which were received by us. This is unique among Chinese corporations. While we are very proud of this, I think Wanda has something more to be proud of, and that is the Wanda Volunteer Organization.

I. "Wanda Volunteers" was the first nationwide corporate volunteer organization established

Early in 1994, Wanda spent considerable efforts to establish the first corporate volunteer organization. Because the China Charity Federation had yet to be established in many places at that time, and corporate volunteer organizations were even fewer, government approval was considered a difficult challenge. Along with Wanda's cross-regional national development in the 1990s, our charity volunteer organization followed in nationwide establishment. As of now, we have 917 volunteer posts across the nation, with more than 100,000 volunteers. I'm afraid that this is also China's largest corporate volunteer organization. Of course there are corporations with more staff than ours, but not necessarily more volunteers than Wanda. In the first half of 2014, there were 697 volunteer events organized by each of the corporation's volunteer posts with 52,715 employees participating.

II. All Wanda Employees are Volunteers

Wanda has a provision on recruiting and hiring staff; if you want to join Wanda, you must automatically commit to participating in volunteer work. If one does not accept this provision, we will not proceed in hiring that person. When renewing the contract, it is the same. Moreover, the requirement is that after becoming a volunteer, one must volunteer at least once a year. This way, all of our staff members become the corporation's volunteers. I believe that along with the development of Wanda as a corporate organization, our volunteers will also continue to increase in numbers.

Most people have basically agreed to this exercise, but there have been a few extremely individual youths who did not approve of this concept. They felt they had come to Wanda to work, so why did they have to do volunteer work? One staff member at a certain project in southern China complained about this, and we had to urge him to back off.

Even though we require everyone to volunteer, we do not advocate that employees donate money. Donations are primarily contributions from the business. Our corporation has a fund, and each year arrangements are made. We have already arranged 400 million yuan in public welfare donations for three consecutive years. Therefore, our request of the staff is just a bit of action, just to volunteer a minimum of once a year. Philanthropy and public welfare are kept alive by persevering with this annual action.

III. Creating the Content of Volunteer Events

How a volunteer organization engages is very important. Volunteer organizations have many approaches. Very early on, our volunteer organization used to do services like picking up litter. Later on, we discovered that these types of events are too arbitrary and have no educational significance for our staff. Then we clarified that we were opting for larger scale "designated help." Each location, and each type of company, whether it was real estate, retail, or cultural industry, should all have a designated aid agency. This way, by persevering over many years, the target would certainly receive help. At that time we were helping the village in Pulandian County in Dalian. Through many years of our help, the per capita income of this village was lifted above the poverty line.

Then there are Wanda volunteer posts, such as the one in Nanning. Because it helps a Hope Primary School year in and year out, and because its activities are done with much verve and enthusiasm, this volunteer post has been named Guangxi Exemplary Volunteer Organization. There is also our Innovative Public Welfare Event "Spiritual Journey," which has been around for almost a decade. In this event, companies in every place visit a poverty-stricken area once. Why do we do so? Overall, we can see that when all is said and done, our businesses are in above-average cities, and employee income is relatively high. Over time, changes take place with regards to our life coordinates, comparison targets, and reference coefficients. We may be seeking a house, money, a career advancement, etc., so each year we ask everyone to visit a poor village and experience a regional disparity, the gap between urban and rural areas that has become so big. Once we had a staff member that wrote an article about the "Spiritual Journey."

This is what the employee had to say:

> 'Beijing Fangshan District is an impoverished village 100 kilometers from CBD Wanda. In places like this you can see the poverty, but it is possible that people living in developed places like Beijing, Shanghai, Chengdu, and Wuhan still don't realize how big China's current regional disparities are. Many places are truly in need of help and need us to do these public welfare activities each year.'

In addition, each year we organize a national volunteer campaign in over 100 cities. Each year there is unified organization and action, like our three-year consecutive school campaign "Caring for Children of Manual Laborers." Why organize this particular volunteer campaign? There is a relationship between this event and the nature of our business. We are in real estate, and 95% of construction workers are from rural areas. The circumstances of the children of migrant workers are quite hard. They generally switch schools once every year or two, there are no people and no funds supporting these schools, the students can't participate in local examinations, and the teaching resources are sorely lacking. Due to these circumstances, we ask that local designated points, as much as possible, help a migrant school. For three consecutive years now we've done the national volunteer campaign "Caring for Children of Manual Workers," and the results are pretty good.

IV. Letting Charity Become Corporate Culture

Why do we view volunteer organizations as so important? It is because we realize that when the corporation donates to charity, if the culture of philanthropy has not been popularized in the corporation, then this matter just becomes a personal activity of the boss; staff members do not understand and support it, and the activity cannot be sustained. So I think what we are after here is allowing the concept of charity to become a common understanding among the vast majority of staff members and to become a kind of culture. Therefore, our corporate website, monthly publication, and mobile news all frequently report on feature volunteer charity events.

Each year 100 outstanding volunteers are selected from the whole group and praised, even given job promotions. In Dalian we had a female employee who relocated her house three times to follow a school for orphans, so she could teach them in her spare time. At first we didn't know about the matter, but later her colleague mentioned it in a speech. Thinking she was a great example, we praised her and directly promoted her by two pay levels.

Every year Wanda comes out with a "Wanda Story," which includes a volunteering story. Each story has a protagonist and photos. So far, Wanda has produced over a dozen annual "Wanda Stories," which are sent out to all employees. Moreover, each year the group's year-end summary sums up the charitable volunteer work, and hopes that charity is an important part of our corporate culture.

I hope that our corporation will be able to develop even further in the future, and will have the ability to contribute more to more people. At the same time, I hope our staff is learning and progressing in our organization, a culture of philanthropy is forming, and everyone is able to maintain, as much as possible, a good heart towards society and a clear conscience.

Chapter Nine

Culture

Wanda's Corporate Culture

6 February, 2012 – A speech at the opening ceremony of Wanda Institute

Wang Jianlin delivered a speech as "the first lesson" of Wanda Institute during the opening ceremony held on 6 February 2012. Wanda Institute is the venue for internal training of middle and senior managers of the Wanda Group. Measuring 128,000 square meters in total, it will be able to accommodate up to 3,000 students once construction is completed, and it is recognized as one of the best schools built by private companies in China.

During the "first lesson," Wang raised high expectations for the school. He talked about the corporate culture of Wanda, and the lecture was attended by over 440 staff members:

They asked me to "teach" the first lesson at the Wanda Institute. At first, I wanted to talk about commercial real estate, but changed the topic to Wanda's corporate culture in the interest of many senior managers here who joined the company recently. It's my second speech on Wanda's corporate culture. I did the first one eight years ago when our corporate culture was upgraded and I explained the system. During the past eight years, the company has expanded further with numerous business model innovations, and our corporate culture too was further developed. My speech today is intended as a summary of the latest changes in the culture of Wanda.

I. Our core values

The central concept of Wanda's corporate culture today is to build the company into an "global centennial brand."

1. What does the core concept mean?

An "global brand" should be understood on three levels, i.e. world-class scale, management and corporate culture. First, our business operations need to be scaled up to an international level. We can't say that our company is a world-class company if its yearly revenue is only a few billion yuan. That would be too small to even rank us among the top 500 Chinese companies. Second, our business management needs to meet international standards. The level of management is critical to the success of a company. Third, our corporate culture should meet international standards.

The aim of building Wanda into a "centennial brand" should be interpreted in the following two ways:

1. An evergreen business. By international standards, companies that last less than ten years are regarded as short-lived enterprises; companies that last 10-30 years are middle-aged; and companies of over 30 years are considered long-lasting. Our ambition is to bring Wanda to the top level of long-lasting enterprises, a company that lasts more than 100 years and so is evergreen. It has been thousands of years since the first exchange of goods occurred in human society. During this period, no companies managed to remain prosperous for more than 200 years, and that's why no company ever aspired to become a millennial enterprise. Companies emerge and die – it's in the nature of things. Companies only last 100 or 200 years at the most, and that's how old companies are replaced by new ones. The evolving nature of businesses inspires and encourages new entrepreneurs to build their own companies. Wanda now owns a lot of properties that produce long-term profits. Buildings constructed with reinforced concrete can survive 100 years easily

without any quality issues. Even if we need to rebuild them a century later, we can do that at limited cost, much cheaper than land acquisition. It would be easy for Wanda to last 100 years as long as we can refrain from making any high-risk investment or committing any major mistakes. We already have an evergreen foundation in place in terms of assets and business model.

2. We should focus on long-term interests. To build Wanda into a company that lasts 100 years, we need to be far-sighted and focus on long-term benefits. We're driven by long-term sustainable cash flow in everything we do now, commercial properties, cultural business and tourism investment alike. Pursuing long-term goals and benefits is our way of doing business. Over ten years ago, many people tried to talk me into investing in coal-mines in Inner Mongolia, and today they ask me to invest in various projects, but I didn't give in to temptation and stuck to industry and commerce. Wanda will never prioritize investment projects or operate financial derivatives. We'll always base our business on industry and commerce. With a close look at the histories of modern companies, you'll find that few companies made it to the Fortune 500 list through investment. Of course, there are exceptionally talented investors such as Warren Buffett, but his company is not a Fortune 500 company. It's nearly impossible to create a world-class enterprise through short-term investment, and fast money won't make you one of the richest men in the world.

2. How our core values evolved over time

The success of Wanda was not achieved overnight. Our corporate culture evolved as the company grew and our vision broadened. The evolution process can be divided into three phases with different priorities.

Phase 1: 1988-1997. During this period, the philosophy of Wanda's corporate culture was to "conduct oneself honestly and handle matters astutely." Integrity is the foundation of our corporate culture. It may sound like nothing more than an ordinary slogan today, but it was a bold move at that time. The real estate market was chaotic back then, before the introduction of the land transfer system. No license was required for property sales, and any company could cash in on real estate projects as long as it had the resources to get land approvals. It could simply sell apartments first and build them with the money paid. The general manager of Xigang Housing Property Development, predecessor of Wanda, was accused of corruption shortly after the establishment of the company, and it ran up large debts of several millions of yuan. The company had a hard time surviving. The district government then made it known that it would give the company to anyone who could save it from bankruptcy and repay the debts. I was the office manager in the Xigang district government and volunteered for the challenge. In early 1989, the company was about to develop the first project. Before the opening, I went on an inspection tour to the sales department. The manager reported that the deputy general manager told her to mark up floor area selling price for every apartment. I asked why? She told me all other companies did it, and most of them had bigger markups than ours. Nobody really cared anyway. I thought it was fraud and stopped it. I told the manager to sell the apartments according to the actual floor area. In retrospect, I realized that companies should be more aware of the importance of business integrity in a marketplace where integrity was seriously lacking. There was a lot of fraud back then, and many consumers had been ripped off. As an old European proverb goes, "fool me once, shame on you; fool me twice, shame on me." As a business, we do not cheat anyone and should not be cheated either, so we asked our employees to "conduct oneself honestly and handle matters astutely." To do conduct oneself honestly means that we should be honest when doing business and developing the company by developing high-quality products; and to handle matters astutely is to remain wary and alert to fraud.

Phase 2: 1998-2001. The core concept of Wanda's corporate culture during this period was "creating wealth together, sharing with society," and corporate social responsibility was defined as the priority. Starting from the end of 1997, Wanda embarked on large-scale cross-regional development, which marked a real landmark in the company's development history. It was through cross-regional development that Wanda gradually became one of the few national property developers in China, and our competitiveness grew to leaps and bounds. During this period, I called on the company to repay society by fulfilling our social responsibilities, in addition to driving business growth. First, we increased charity donations in proportion to business growth. The larger we grew, the more we should donate. Our charity donations have continued to increase by the year ever since. Second, employee care and environmental protection were gradually added to Wanda's commitment to corporate social responsibilities, and a complete social responsibility system was created. In particular, we have always been an honest taxpayer as a central requirement regarding the fulfillment of our social responsibilities. We took great pride in paying increased taxes every year.

Phase 3: 2002 to date. During this period, the core concept of Wanda's corporate culture was to develop the company into a "global centennial brand," highlighting our pursuit of excellence. Our corporate culture was upgraded in 2006. At that time, the total assets of Wanda exceeded 10 billion yuan, and our annual revenue was nearly 10 billion. We were already one of the most established real estate developers in the country. Some of my friends ... including bosses of some other companies ... told me that it was time to relax and enjoy life, as I had more money than I could possibly spend in my entire life. Identifying business development with "making money to enjoy life" – this is a "glass ceiling" commonly seen among private business owners in China. I once talked with the Wenzhou City mayor. He told me that there were many millionaires and even billionaires in Jiangsu and Zhejiang, but few business owners had more than 10 billion yuan. Why? The reason was that most of them believed that the ultimate goal of business development and wealth accumulation was to make life more enjoyable for themselves and satisfy personal needs, so they lost motivation after their personal wealth grew to several billion yuan. Of course, there's nothing wrong in making personal enjoyment the ultimate goal for business development, but it's not a noble cause to fight for. Should Wanda continue to scale up? And in which direction? These were the main topics of our meetings during this period. We finally reached a consensus through numerous discussions – that is, we needed to build Wanda into a "global centennial brand" ... to make the company a long-lasting enterprise. We'll continue to guide ourselves by this goal for many years to come, until Wanda becomes a truly world-class company. There is no universally recognized definition of world-class enterprises, but I think a world-class company should rank among the largest 100 companies globally in all core indicators. Wanda was created with great ambitions, which have been driving us in our pursuit of excellence. And that is what has made us into a successful business today. All excellent enterprises were created with the "DNA for success" during their very conception.

II. A complete corporate cultural system at Wanda

The success of Wanda is principally attributable to its excellent corporate culture. Our corporate culture is not only limited to the core values, or to the basic code of conduct printed on our employees' handbook. The company has built a complete system of corporate culture, developed, enriched and evolved over the years.

1. Ideology

The ideological system of Wanda's corporate culture comprises core values, fundamental values, corporate visions, etc. The visions are further divided into short-term, medium-term and long-term goals. Our long-term goal is to build the company into a world-class enterprise; medium-term goals are laid down in five-year plans; and short-term goals in annual plans. One of the greatest strengths of Wanda's corporate culture is that we have well-defined development goals. Furthermore, our visions are reviewed and adapted every three to five years, according to the company's progress. At Wanda, we have a fully developed management system in place, involving our internal monthly publications, websites and the employee handbook. They are all building blocks of our ideological system. Take the "management system culture" for example. I started building the enterprise system for Wanda more than 20 years ago. When I took over the company, it was such a mess. Some employees were paid monthly salaries without working, and some were paid overtime without working overtime. We had two company cars, but the drivers used them for moonlighting during office hours. The general managers could not find the drivers when they needed to use the cars. I'd seen all sorts of weird things. In short, the company was a total mess. In the first week I was there, I formulated the *Regulations for Reinforcing Work Discipline* to tighten up on management. During the last decade, management regulations at Wanda were reviewed and amended every two years to add new models and methods, and delete outdated ones. In particular, the 2012 version that we developed in the second half of last year was a third shorter, but the regulations were more actionable and effective. Other companies were keen on every amended version. They used all means at their disposal to get a copy of our latest regulations. Some of them even adopted our regulations without changing a word.

2. Corporate culture system

Wanda's corporate culture system can be summarized with the following four aspects: planning at the beginning of the year, summary at the end of the year, effective budgeting and annual training appraisal. Planning and summary are self-explanatory. We have held annual conferences throughout the past 20 years, and most personal commendation items were cancelled as our business continued to grow which resulted in increasing time constraints during annual conferences. Even speeches by staff representatives were cut to only five minutes. The only thing that remained unchanged over the years was commendations of outstanding group correspondents. This reflects our emphasis on corporate culture. "Effective budgeting" means that Wanda draws up annual budgets for cultural events, staff training and even charity donations. I've established a personal charity fund and will set up a professional organization for charity operations. "Annual training appraisal" means that Wanda attaches great importance to staff training, and the training outcome is summarized in annual meetings every year. In short, at Wanda, corporate culture development is not done arbitrarily, but conducted under a complete set of well-defined institutional arrangements.

3. Organizational system

The corporate culture department of Wanda was established more than ten years ago. It is responsible for the internal monthly publication, the company's websites and publication of Wanda Stories. In addition to Wanda Group, project companies, the commercial property management company, department stores and Wanda Cinemas all have their own publications and websites, and every basic-level company nominates an employee as the "Wanda cultural correspondent" – these initiatives join to form the organizational system of Wanda's corporate culture. Of course, at the end of the day the boss is the most decisive factor for the development of corporate culture. And the boss's support is indispensable to the successful development of our corporate culture at Wanda.

III. Main characteristics of Wanda's corporate culture

Corporate culture is an ideological system. That said, it inevitably manifests itself in concrete physical forms, and excellent companies acquire unique cultural identities. Wanda's corporate culture has taken on eight main characteristics developed over the years:

1. The enterprising spirit

The enterprising spirit is the most salient characteristic of the corporate culture at Wanda. The development of history is a process of constant innovations. We owe our success, first and foremost, to the enterprising spirit and its actions.

We were the first real estate developer in China to succeed in urban redevelopment projects. Wanda was to be a small firm when it was founded in 1988. Back then, "planned quotas" were required for all real estate projects. Property developers had to obtain quotas before applying for land acquisition. The quotas were all allocated by the National Planning Commission, and only the three state-owned developers in Dalian were allocated quotas. Wanda was not one of them, so we had to buy quotas from them. It was like "seeking survival in the cracks." I went to the Dalian government and told them that we would accept any project as long as the profit was enough to sustain ourselves, regardless of location. At that time, there was a shantytown on

Beijing Street to the north of where the municipal government was located. Dozens of households had to share a single water tap and a public toilet. The whole place stank for days each time the toilet was dug. Because of its proximity to the municipal government, it was viewed as a source of shame for the entire city. The government repeatedly asked the three state-owned property developers to redevelop the area, but none were willing to take it. Having heard what I asked for, the government offered to approve planning quotas if I accepted the shantytown project. We estimated that the cost of development of the shantytown project on Beijing Street was 1,200 yuan per square meter, but back then the most expensive apartments in Dalian were priced at 1,100. To make the project profitable, we had to find a way of selling the apartments at 1,500. We made a number of innovations.

1. We decided to fit all apartments with aluminium windows, which were rare in north-eastern China in those days. 2. All apartments came with security doors, which had barely become mainstream in the local housing market. 3. In those days, virtually no living rooms were bright, so we made bright living rooms standard in our design. 4. Toilets used to be a luxury enjoyed only by cadres at the county level or above, but every apartment in the Beijing Street project had a separate toilet. 5. Department-level government officials were entitled to live in 70 square meter apartments, and bureau-level officials lived in 90 square meter apartments. By contrast, the biggest three-bedroom apartments in the Beijing Street project were 130-140 square meters. These five measures may not sound like a big deal today, but they were "nuclear weapons" back then. All the 1,000 odd apartments were sold out even before the relocation had been completed, at a record average price of 1,600 yuan/square meter. Wanda thus became the first company in China with experience in urban redevelopment, offering a new approach to corporate development.

We pioneered the construction quality reward reform for construction companies. In 1990, we started developing a housing project on Minzheng Street, Dalian. According to the state's policy, two yuan was awarded per square meter to construction companies for every municipal-level high quality project built, and four yuan for provincial-level high quality projects. To incentivize them to ensure best construction quality, we increased the rewards by three to five times. As a result, the Minzheng Street project became the first housing development in China that received top ratings across all quality metrics.

We are the first Chinese property developer to pioneer cross-regional project development. In 1993, Wanda went outside Dalian and ventured into the real estate market in Guangdong. At that time, they said "Guangdong is the best place to make money." Northerners were all country bumpkins in the eyes of Guangdong people. It was a great achievement for a company from the north to successfully develop a property project in Guangzhou. We managed to complete several thousand apartments, and sold them all at a profit, albeit a small one. More importantly, we acquired valuable experience in cross-regional development.

We are the first commercial property developer in China. Wanda debuted in commercial real estate development in 2000. Now, more than a decade later, we are a world-class real estate giant operating more than nine million square meters of commercial properties, which will increase to 13 million square meters this year. We currently rank as the fourth-largest real estate operator in the world, and the company is well on track to take over the No. 1 ranking by 2015.

We are the first large-scale investor in cultural businesses. The Wanda Group is the first private enterprise in China to invest in the cultural industry, and the largest investor in cultural businesses among all Chinese companies. In August last year, I reported to leaders of the central government on Wanda's cultural business development, and our achievements were regarded as positively by the leaders.

We are the first deluxe hotel management brand in China. China has developed "two nuclear bombs and one satellite," but still doesn't have a luxury hotel management company of its own. The luxury hotel market is completely dominated by foreign brands. Unfazed, Wanda decided to set up its own luxury hotel management company and make it the pride of the Chinese nation. We believe the company will get a firm foothold on the market in five years. After about ten years, it will be a formidable competitor even for multinational hotel brands.

2. Business integrity

Honesty and integrity are at the core of Wanda's corporate culture.

We developed the Minzheng Street housing project in Dalian in 1990. At that time, the construction quality of housing properties was generally poor, but we were determined to build the project to the highest standard and asked the four construction companies to meet the municipal-level quality requirements for all the buildings, but they refused to cooperate. The government's policy was that construction companies would have their qualifications upgraded if their work was certified to meet municipal-level quality requirements, so why would they turn us down on such a seemingly good deal? After research, we learned that to conform to municipal-level quality standards, the construction company needed to spend an extra 10 yuan per square meter, and if the project was to meet the provincial standards, the extra cost was 20 yuan. State regulations, however, awarded only two yuan for meeting municipal quality standards, and four yuan for provincial quality standards. In other words, the higher the construction quality, the greater the losses they would incur. In view of this, we introduced our own reward mechanism: construction companies would get 10 yuan per square meter if their work met the municipal requirements, and 20 if the work conformed to the provincial standards. All of the four companies accepted the deal, but we were told by the municipal construction committee that the policy violated state rules. We explained that it was intended as an incentive for good construction quality and would be implemented only within Wanda. They finally agreed not to fine us. The incentive scheme worked well. Four of the buildings in the Minzheng Street project were rated municipal-level high quality constructions, and the other four were high quality at provincial level. Two of them especially were commended as "model constructions" in Liaoning Province, making the project the first housing development with the highest ratings on all quality metrics. The construction department of Liaoning Province organized local real estate developers and construction companies to go on a study tour of the project. The first "China Quality Long March" was jointly sponsored by Chinese ministries and commissions under the central government in 1992 to expose quality issues across the country. The organizers carried out inspections in Dalian and were shocked by the high quality of the Minzheng Street project. They even visited the local residents in secret, and all the respondents had high opinions of the project. Although there was no precedent for commending individual companies throughout the history of the event, the organizers decided to make an exception and award the only "high quality housing properties" medal to the Minzheng Street project. We've always committed ourselves to high quality and competitive pricing and were recognized as the "builder of high quality apartments" in the real estate market in Dalian.

In early 1996, Wanda took the lead in announcing the "three guarantees" among all Chinese property developers: (1) a guarantee against any leakage – we'd compensate 30,000 Yaun for any leak; (2) a guarantee that the actual area matches that indicated on the property ownership certificate – otherwise, we'd pay three times the difference between the stated and actual area size; (3) a guarantee that properties can be unconditionally returned or refunded within 60 days after construction had completed. Many of my colleagues objected to the leakage guarantee. I understood that no developer could completely eliminate water leakage in 1,000 or more apartments, but at least we should minimize it as much as we could for our customers. The "three guarantees" were first implemented in the Changchun Garden project, and the leakage rate was low thanks to effective regulations and management. Leakage occurred in only a few apartments out of nearly 1,000. People worried about the 60-day unconditional return and refund policy. What if all the buyers returned their flats and claimed the refund? The worries proved to be unfounded, and only less than ten buyers asked for a refund. After the successful experiment, Wanda introduced the "three guarantee" policy to all other projects. The aim was to blaze a trail and beat the competition. After the government "rectification" in 1993, the overall profitability of the real estate industry slid into the red, and many developers disappeared. How did Wanda manage to increase its market share and achieve business growth in the face of the extreme difficulties? The secret to our success is quality-oriented initiatives – such as the "three guarantees". When we started to set up branches on a nationwide scale in 1998, we had a quarter share of the real estate market in Dalian. Our "three guarantees" policy was a sensational success across the country, and received extensive positive media coverage. In June 2000, the Ministry of Construction, China Consumer Association and four other government organizations held a meeting at the Great Hall of the People, attended by over 1,000 real estate developers, to promote Wanda's experience in property quality assurance. I made a keynote speech during the meeting. The organizers called on all participants to ensure property quality following Wanda's example. The then construction minister, Yu Zhengsheng, was present at the meeting. He praised our company highly and made Wanda the first and only model real estate developer ever announced by the Ministry of Construction.

In 2003, we developed the Wanda Plaza on Tai Yuan Street in Shenyang, and about 350 stores were sold. As we only had limited experience in commercial property development back then, we made mistakes in design. Consequently, the stores didn't attract large traffic and suffered poor sales. We decided to charter the stores in the interests of small property owners, and hired experienced department store managers to locate the problems. We tried to come up with solutions. At first, we added a roof and central heating to the shopping street to solve the issue of the cold in winter. Then we connected the stores with the underground facilities, installing many elevators that cost us tens of millions of yuan. Several times we changed the team responsible for attracting tenants… Nothing seemed to fundamentally work. By 2007, we had a better understanding of commercial real estate development. After several brainstorm sessions, we found that there were serious inherent mistakes in the plaza design that couldn't be remedied unless the buildings were redesigned and rebuilt. Some store owners sued us and demanded a refund. Several dozens of lawsuits were filed against us, but both the intermediate courts and the higher courts in Shenyang and Liaoning ruled in favor of our company. Most companies would just walk away, but we were interested in the long-term growth of the commercial real estate business, so we decided to rebuild the plaza in line with our commitment as a responsible developer for investors. The plaza was reconstructed in 2008, and re-opened in 2009. The stores all had a booming business. We only earned 610 million yuan from store sales, but it cost us one billion yuan to buy back the stores, in addition to the demolition and reconstruction costs of 1.5 billion yuan. This story should be told and told again as a classic example of our commitment to business integrity. It had a much broader impact than the "refrigerator incident" at Haier – they just smashed a few dozen of refrigerators, but we tore down 350 stores. The Haier incident was nowhere near comparable to ours. Not to mention that we bought back the stores in early 2008 when we had severe financial difficulties. When we distributed the compensation, many of the owners were moved to tears. Many of them refused to take the money and promised to buy more stores if Wanda would build more in Shenyang. Our decision to rebuild the plaza in Shenyang was unprecedented, and will unlikely be repeated by any other company. It is remembered as a real landmark in Wanda's "business integrity" campaign.

In recognition of its commitment to honesty in doing business, Wanda was named by the government and the national real estate industry association as the most trustworthy property developer in China for many consecutive years. In 2007, the Ministry of Construction and China Real Estate Association held the national real estate trustworthy business conference, and Wanda was invited to give a keynote speech to share its successful experience.

3. Environmental protection

In 2000, Wanda developed one of the first energy-saving housing projects in China, Yong Jing Tai in Dalian. Although the government had not issued any environmental protection regulations back then, we applied external wall insulation and advanced architectural and lighting design technologies, and achieved an energy saving rate of 65% for the project. In winter, the temperature in Dalian drops way below -10°C, but the apartments of the Yong Jing Tai project do not need any central heating. Following the successful completion of the project, we launched another eco-friendly housing project in Dalian, Hua Fu, in 2004. A few years later, the property management team found that approximately 50% of the residents don't buy central heating during winter months. As heating consumption is measured separately for individual apartments, that means about half of the apartments are warm enough without central heating.

In 2003, we developed the Wanda Star City in Nanchang, in Jiangxi Province. Measuring more than one million square meters in total area, it was our first housing project to apply external wall insulation in a southern Chinese city (i.e. located to the south of the Yangtze River). Adoption of the energy-saving technology received positive results, and the Wanda Star City was selected as the model energy-saving project by Jiangxi Province.

In 2003, we developed Dianchi Satellite City in Kunming. Due to its location close to Dianchi Lake, we conducted an environmental impact assessment. Although environmental assessment was not required by the government in 2003, we knew that the lake was badly polluted and couldn't bear any extra burden. Wanda thus became the first property developer in China to do environmental impact assessment on its own initiative. In addition, the project was equipped with sewage and rainwater collection facilities such that no pollution was caused to the surrounding environment.

Wanda is the national leader in "green building" construction. As of 2011, Wanda had 16 Wanda Plazas and two hotels certified for green building design. In particular, the two hotels were certified for green building operations. I made it a rule that, in future, all Wanda Plazas and hotels be certified for green building design and operation, of which the latter is more challenging to obtain. But while the two hotels have made it, so should other Wanda hotels. In addition to green building construction, from 2013 onward all our housing properties for sale will have been fitted up. Not only can significant savings be made with centralized fitting up, but the public awareness of environmental protection can be enhanced. This cannot be achieved overnight, but takes many years of consistent dedication and hard work.

4. Employee care

First of all, our employees are the best paid in their respective professions among all Chinese companies. Our human resources department conducts a wage survey every two years, and staff's wages are adjusted accordingly to make sure that the wages are in the top bracket for any given profession nationwide. We're the first company in China to adopt a seniority-based wage system. For every year employees work for the company, they will get a monthly increment of 100 yuan, making a yearly total of an extra 1,200 yuan. In other words, after you have worked in the company for ten years, you'll receive 12,000 yuan every year as seniority bonus alone. Therefore, an annual pay rise is guaranteed at Wanda. Our senior managers are competitively paid, and some of them receive stock options.

Secondly, we really care about the well-being of our employees. Wanda introduced the paid leave system ten years ago, and every employee is entitled to four days' paid leave every quarter; the company pays for one medical check every year for the employees and buys gym cards for those working in the headquarters. It is a rule at Wanda that all basic-level branches should have their own canteens to be operated by the branches themselves to ensure food safety. Two years ago, we launched the paid holiday scheme for outperforming employees. Selected employees can stay in Wanda hotels across China for free, and two return flight tickets are reimbursed by the company.

Thirdly, we always attach great emphasis to staff training. A large number of training courses are offered every year. We built the Wanda Institute with an investment of over 700 million yuan, and internal training at Wanda has been taken to a higher level as a result. As I said: Wanda's employees earn more, learn more and enjoy more.

5. Charity

First, since day one we have emphasized charity work. Charity is a tradition here. Within two years of the company's foundation in 1988, we donated one million Yuan to the teachers' kindergarten in Xigang, Dalian; in 1992, we donated 2.8 million yuan to replace the hard covering at Dalian People's Square with lawns; in 1994, we donated 20 million yuan to the Xigang Stadium construction project.

Second, charity is a systematic undertaking at Wanda. Every year, we work out an annual charity budget and review it at the end of the year. We release corporate social responsibility reports on a yearly basis.

Third, charity is part of our corporate culture. This is because it has been consistently supported by top management. If employees do charity work well, they will be promoted and rewarded. There have been numerous cases of charity deeds among our employees. For example, every Wanda employee joining the Communist Party is required to make donations to a poor child attending school, and this has become an unwritten rule in the company. Local branches are required to organize a "spiritual journey" every year, and every staff member should volunteer at least once every year.

6. To be the best

We have lofty ambitions and enforce extremely strict requirements for every piece of work. We believe in finishing "every piece of work to the highest standard possible." If we positioned our company as an average Chinese company, we would have developed only two Wanda Plazas every year, rather than 20. Two would have been enough. But our goal is to make Wanda a world-class enterprise. We want to compete with state-owned enterprises through our hard work. If the current trend continues, in 2015 Wanda's annual revenue will exceed 200 billion yuan; our assets will grow to 300 billion yuan, annual taxes 30 billion yuan, and net profit in the range of tens of billions of yuan. We will rank as the No. 1 Chinese company, except for a few state-owned monopolies. We rely only on ourselves and market-based growth, so we deserve more respect from others. Once Wanda has entered a market – whatever it is, no one else can be the leader in China, or even the world. To this end, every one of us needs to be the best player in the field.

7. Powerful execution capability

Wanda's strong execution capability is widely recognized among peer companies as well as the government and consumers. We have turned "the impossible" into reality, time and time again. I held talks with a foreign delegation a few days ago. One of the delegates was the chairman of a well-known investment company based in the U.S. Everyone asked me the same question: How could Wanda possibly launch 20 shopping malls every year, with dozens more in construction? It would be simply impossible for foreign companies. Their minds would be boggled if I told them that some of the plazas were built in less than one year. The strength of Wanda's execution capability is attributable to the following three factors:

First, we always live up to our word. While building the Wanda Plaza in Baiyun(Guangzhou), we promised the local government that we'd complete the construction before the Asian Games, but the land was delivered by the government five months behind schedule. We managed to make it up through meticulous planning and hard work. In the end, we built the plaza in merely 11 months and delivered it ahead of schedule. The project was a sensational success. The government officials were impressed. With their help, we signed six contracts during the investment conference held in Guangdong in March last year, and two of them have already begun. Were it not for the successful construction of the Baiyun Wanda Plaza, the government leaders in Guangdong wouldn't have invited us to develop local projects. We have earned ourselves a name in Guangdong as an efficient developer.

We completed building the Chu River and Han Street project in the central cultural district in Wuhan in ten months, without sacrificing the construction quality in the least. On the contrary, it has proven to be of impressive quality. By the end of the year, a Madame Tussauds store, an Apple flagship store and a host of famous restaurants will be opened there, making the street a more fascinating place to visit. The No. 1 flagship of Wanda Plaza, Han Street Wanda Plaza, will be launched in June next year, together with the largest and best quality Wanda Cinema in China. In 2014, Han Street will become the "No. 1 street in China" after the launch of the two cultural projects within the central cultural district. It may even be called the "No.1 street in the world." There won't be another street as diverse as Han Street in the world.

Second, we insist on accurate planning and effective land acquisition. We start the development of every project with accurate planning, design and cost estimates, before we decide whether to acquire the land or not. Through modular management, we keep all expenses and cash flow strictly within the budget throughout the project development process. Of all of the more than 30 projects we delivered last year, the costs were kept below the present targets, and profits were all above the targets without a single exception. We plan with absolute precision and get every piece of land that we want. This is the key to our success.

Third, we have effective discipline enforcement. This is our trademark. We are relentless when it comes to discipline enforcement. Even if the vice president breaks the rules, the same discipline applies. Iron discipline gives our team its strong execution capability.

8. Promoting traditional Chinese culture

Culture is passed down from generation to generation. All Chinese companies have a Chinese cultural identity, and so it is important that they pass on this cultural heritage. At Wanda, we pay particular attention to the promotion of traditional Chinese culture. In 2005, we recommended The Analects by Confucius to all employees, and organized theme studies, debates and lectures throughout the year. It was years before Yu Dan's *The Analects* lecture series aired by China Central Television (CCTV). I started collecting Chinese calligraphy and paintings 25 years ago, and have been holding an art exhibition every year ever since to support talented Chinese artists. Several years ago, Wanda invited famous etiquette experts to give our employees training on manners to improve the overall staff quality. Wanda takes cultural heritage seriously, and that's in part what makes it the successful business that it is today. A company won't achieve much if it has lost its cultural roots.

IV. Wanda has a diverse range of cultural activities

Culture is a spiritual thing, which must be made tangible through concrete physical forms. The corporate culture of Wanda is reflected through ten regular cultural events, although the events are not an exhaustive list of everything the corporate culture embodies.

1. One website and one monthly publication – the core media for spreading Wanda's corporate culture.

2. One good book every year – I recommend a good book to the employees at the beginning of every year.

3. One speech contest every year – the speeches are compiled with photos of the winners to stimulate enthusiasm among staff members.

4. One Wanda Stories every year – touching stories that happened at Wanda are collected and published internally.

5. Staff sports events are organized once a year.

6. Every employee works as a volunteer for at least one hour and at least once every year, to raise the staff's awareness of their social responsibilities.

7. One spiritual journey every year – every company holds a poverty alleviation event every year, in which the employees go to the poorest town, village, etc. nearby. Most of our employees work in modern office buildings, have a good income, live in their own apartments and drive decent cars. A comfortable life may make them blind to the immense gap between the rich and the poor in China. The aim of the spiritual journey is to purify our soul and thoughts.

8. One corporate social responsibility report every year.

9. One holiday paid by the company – we started the paid holiday program for selected outperforming employees two years ago.

10. One grand annual conference. The annual conference is the prime venue for promoting Wanda's corporate culture. Every year, the employees scramble to get a seat in the conference. As the number of our employees has kept increasing, there are only three ways left now to take part in the event: (1) Senior managers at or above the general manager level; (2) selected outperforming employees; (3) performers included in the program. In short, only people who have achieved something can take part in the annual conference. We have held 22 annual conferences since 1989, without interruption. This is a marvellous achievement in itself. Ten years ago, we debated during management board meetings whether the annual conference should be held, and how the performances should be arranged. Some managers objected, saying that they'd rather have a day off or we shouldn't take the performances too seriously. But we decided to hold the conference every year, and every performance must be of very high quality. We have abided by the decision for the past 22 years. The appeal of the event has increased by the year.

V. The great role of Wanda's corporate culture

Corporate culture is not just for appearances. The key is that it is useful in itself.

1. A shared corporate identity

Wanda's corporate values have very broad application. For example, we ask our commercial property management company to prioritize "safety, service and quality" in all of their operations. Profitability of the tenants is given precedence over the property management company's own profits. The central idea is to make our partners profitable, but this is only one of the many aspects of Wanda's corporate values.

Our core values...I summed it up as follows: people come before material things; the company's values come before the individual employees; and social values come before the company.

People: Wanda always prioritizes human resources, which are regarded as our most valuable asset. People have the highest value. Our human-resources department works with dozens of external head hunters. The top priority for top-level managers of all business lines is to find suitable talent. Nothing is insurmountable as long as we have the right people.

Company values: We respect every individual staff member, but the values of the company are more important than those of individual employees, i.e. employees should subordinate their personal interests to arrangements made by the company. For example, Wanda has set up many local branches across China. The employees must comply with the company's decision, and can't insist on working only in cities such as Beijing or Shanghai, if the company needs them to relocate to other areas.

Social values: It is Wanda's ultimate goal to become a "responsible corporate citizen." The development of our company should drive society to advance, benefiting all of its members.

All our employees identify with these core values. We were voted the "best employer" in a survey broadcast by CCTV. The survey was conducted by an overseas research company. As the results show, Wanda's employees had the highest degree of identification with the company's corporate culture, development vision and corporate image, far outshining all other well-known Chinese companies. We scored more than 80 out of 100 points on all criteria, and our average score was 20 points higher than the second-best. Team cohesion can be achieved only if the employees can identify with the company's vision and corporate values. Longer-serving employees at Wanda tend to be more hard-working, and more willing to sacrifice themselves for the sake of the company – this is because they have been steeped longer in the corporate culture.

2. Stronger team cohesion

Corporate culture benefits the company the most in terms of enhanced corporate cohesion and employee loyalty. We conducted a study on staff turnover in the first half of last year. Our findings show that between 2006 and 2010, the turnover rate of Wanda's senior managers was 6.2%, but many of the managers left were dismissed from their jobs. Of them, 80% left the company within one year of joining, and the turnover rate among senior managers working in the company for more than three years was as low as 1.2%. At Yangcheng Lake, some crabs are brought from other places to live in the lake for a couple of weeks, and then they are caught and sold as local crabs (crabs from the Yangcheng Lake are famous in China and more expensive than other varieties). These crabs are called "bathing crabs," i.e. they're put into the lake to pretend to be local crabs). By analogy, most of the managers who left are like the "bathing crabs." Joking aside, they're not really our people. Today, our senior managers are highly sought after by head hunters, but the turnover rate is very low among senior managers working with Wanda for more than three years, and it's even lower among core management team members. This attests to the strong team cohesion within the company.

3. Improved competitiveness

Business competition can be divided into five categories: product competition, price competition, quality competition, brand competition and cultural competition. The first two of them are at the lowest level; quality and brand based competition are at a higher level; and the last one, competition focused on corporate culture, is the most advanced form of competition.

At the level of product competition, the key is to create products that the competitors don't have; for price competition, the focus is to minimize costs; quality competition focuses on the ability to produce higher quality products at the same competitive price; brand competition is a higher form of competition, where the key factors are customer loyalty and product differentiation. In Europe, many families have been using the same auto brands (e.g. Mercedes-Benz and BMW) for several generations. Many of the football teams there have more than 100 years of history. Many families remained loyal fans of the same teams generation after generation, even after the teams have been relegated from League A to League B, or from League B to League C. But the families go to their matches and cheer for them all the same. This is what loyalty means. The factor is product differentiation. Toyota and Honda are both automakers, but everyone knows that they are distinctly different from each other. In fact, their products, i.e. cars, are similar, but there are major differences between the two brands in terms of product design, marketing, service and corporate culture. The most advanced form of competition, competition on corporate culture, occurs on the spiritual level. At this level, competition is hardly perceivable. Wanda is currently at the stage of brand competition, below the level of cultural competition, which is our ultimate goal.

At Wanda, our efforts to build on our competitiveness are made in the following two respects. (1) Strengthening competitiveness through rapid business growth. We achieved three major types of progress in three years: our revenue grew from 43 billion yuan in 2009 to 77 billion in 2010 and to 105 billion in 2011. We have an advanced business model, but this is not the only reason behind our explosive business growth. There are at least more than 100 shopping center developers, 200-300 hotel operators and over 130 cinema companies in China. A powerful corporate culture is what sets us apart from the competitors and makes us grow substantially faster. It offers a foundation for our rapid business development. (2) Consolidating our competitive advantages. Our mission is to make Wanda the absolute leader in the world in shopping mall development, 5-star hotel operations, cultural businesses and resort tourism by 2020. In addition, we will be the leading department store operator at least in China, and will compete with foreign department stores on the global markets as the next step. Behind our ambitious goals, we derive our confidence from our strong competitive advantages. In addition to our business model, execution capability and financial strengths, Wanda's competitive advantages are founded in our corporate culture – our pursuit of achieving excellence. By the end of the year, Wanda will rank among the Fortune 500 companies by all financial standards, and that's why we proposed to build the company into a leading world-class enterprise. By 2020, if we manage to make Wanda the world's leader in all our business sectors, we will have fulfilled our target.

In the future, I'll give two speeches at Wanda Institute every year, and I hope to share with you the most valuable experiences that I have had during the development of Wanda. Hopefully the external lecturers can share their valuable insights with you, and make the Wanda Institute an even greater success.

Thank you!

Chapter Ten

Asset-Light

Wanda's Model is Light in Assets

15 April, 2015 – A lecture at Shenzhen Stock Exchange

During the eighth entrepreneurship forum of the Shenzhen Stock Exchange (SZSE) held on April 15, Wanda Group Chairman Wang Jianlin gave a keynote speech entitled "The Asset-Light Model at Wanda", where he elaborated for the first time on the Group's asset-light strategy.

Below is the transcribed speech:

As a leading world-class estate developer, Wanda now boasts the largest properties (measured in combined floor area) under management all around the globe. Revolving around property development, we have expanded our business presence into many other sectors. The company has embarked on a full-scale transition since last year, based on analyses of the future trends in the real estate industry: from a geographical perspective, we are driving a shift in the company toward a multinational enterprise; in terms of business lines, the company is in the midst of a transition from a property-oriented enterprise toward a high-tech service supplier. Today, I will focus my speech on the transition of Wanda's core business – commercial real estate.

1. The asset-light strategy at Wanda

What is asset-heavy? The city complex is the main product of Wanda Commercial Properties. This product model starts with the construction of a large Wanda Plaza, supplemented with auxiliary properties such as offices, retail stores and apartments, whereby the supporting properties are sold and the resulting proceeds are invested in the Wanda Plaza for long-term operations. The absence of long-term property investment financial products in China means that Wanda has to rely on property sales for its leasing business. All Wanda Plazas are owned and managed by the company itself, and it also receives full rental revenues – this model is called asset-heavy.

And what is asset-light? It is a different model where the construction of Wanda Plazas is funded exclusively by external investors, and Wanda takes care of site selection, project design and construction, tenant attraction and property management, leveraging the brand appeal of Wanda Plaza and its unique "Huiyun" intelligent business information management system. With this model, the rental income is shared between Wanda and the investors according to a certain distribution ratio. We started developing this totally new model (namely asset-light Wanda Plaza) last year, and have put it into practice now.

Going forward, Wanda will move toward the asset-light model. As of the end of 2014, a total of 109 Wanda Plazas have been opened, with 26 new projects due to open in 2015, bringing the total area of properties under management to over 25 million square meters. All of the new plazas this year will be operated under the asset-heavy model – given the three-year construction cycle involving site selection, negotiations, architectural design, land purchase and opening, it is impossible to apply the asset-light model to the new projects in 2015. However, of the 50 plazas planned for 2016, more than 20 will be developed and operated as "light assets". From 2017 onward, we will keep opening at least 50 new plazas every year, and over 40 of them will be asset-light. Of the 90 million square meters of our existing land reserve, over 20 million are planned as self-owned properties, and 70 million are developed for sale. We plan to digest these 70 million square meters of properties within five years. In other words, "heavy assets" will disappear from Wanda Plazas, meaning that Wanda Commercial Properties make the transition from a real estate developer to a business investment service operator – similar to hotel management companies – featuring fully asset-light operations.

2. What caused the asset-light transition?

Wanda's asset-heavy business has been performing well and has good potential for future growth. Urbanization is still in full swing in China, and the Wanda model has been copied by many property companies. So why did you decide to move toward asset-light?

(1) To increase our competitiveness

With 135 Wanda Plazas in operation by the end of 2015, we will be the largest commercial real estate developer in the world. It would be an achievement big enough for us to become complacent. Sit back and relax and watch property leasing grow naturally. But we have more ambitious goals – relative to a market with nearly 1.4 billion consumers, our market share is still too small, and we must continue to scale up to consolidate our competitive edge. The asset-heavy model is inherently influenced by the cyclical nature of the property industry. During a property boom, it is very easy to increase sales and maintain a healthy capital flow as well as driving business growth. However, we believe the Chinese real estate industry has come to a turning point in terms of supply and demand, and the era of huge profit has come to an end. Going forward, property developers must achieve high standard branding, pricing, marketing, etc. operations to survive in the marketplace. There is still room for the asset-heavy model to develop further, but it is confronting increasing challenges. The asset-light strategy is the answer to scaling up our businesses. The Wanda Plaza brand has a solid reputation. Many organizations and individual investors have come to us asking for investment opportunities. It is an opportunity too good to miss. As the fashionable saying goes, the best business is to do your business with investments from others. We aim to grow bigger and bigger during the next five years and beat all our competitors. We are building a wider and deeper "moat" for the Wanda brand.

(2) To tap into markets in small/medium-size cities

Some analysts asked me why shouldn't Wanda keep focusing on tier one and two cities? Are housing prices and rents high enough in tier three and four cities? This represents a misperception about the real estate business. The most important indicator in property development is not the housing price or rent per square meter. Rather it is the rental yield, i.e. the ratio of rent to investment (the annual rental revenue after deducting taxes divided by total property development). In this respect, property projects in tier one and two cities may even be inferior to those in tier three and four cities, because the former entails greater land costs and heavier investments.

The housing price is the primary consideration in the asset-heavy model, where investment is limited only to projects with high sales profits. This would keep us out of tier three and four markets. By contrast, the asset-light model only involves pure investment without property sales, whereby investment can be made in projects as long as the local urban population is large enough to maintain a reasonable rental yield. This enables us to enter the local markets of many tier three and four cities. The biggest challenge in these markets lies in how to attract retailer occupants, and such a barrier prevents most developers from entering these cities. For us, retailer resources happen to be one of our biggest competitive advantages – we have more than 5,000 contracted retailers, many of whom have close business ties with us and follow Wanda wherever we go. In fact, we do not attract retailers, but select them. As a zero tolerance rule, in any given year, a Wanda Plaza retailer cannot open more stores than 50% of the number of Wanda Plazas opened that year – the number was lowered even further to 33% last year. This is a precaution against potential risks – if 500 Wanda Plazas are opened in total and all of the properties available for a particular business (supermarkets, for example) are leased to the same retailer, it would put the entire operation at risk if the retailer encounters business difficulties. Secondly, such a rule also prevents corruption. Bribing our retailer business managers will not give the retailer unlimited access to stores at Wanda Plazas. We have worked out the maximum number of stores allowed for each brand.

The relatively cheap land supplies in tier three and four cities allow us to select favorable locations. From our experience, a tier three or four city with 400,000-500,000 local residents is totally capable of supporting a large-scale Wanda Plaza. Furthermore, consumers in these cities tend to have higher brand loyalty.

Through years of real estate operations, we found that commercial property investment in China is currently in a state of development imbalance, where the markets are over-saturated in major cities, whereas investment in tier three cities and some popular tier four cities has remained scarce. Many of them don't even have a multiplex cinema, let alone large city complexes. Judging by our revenue statistics alone, 70% revenue growth is contributed by tier three to four cities. Despite relatively low spending per customer, the combined population in these cities and high customer loyalty make it easier to establish Wanda Plaza as the central business center. In addition, properties in these cities offer a return on investment more or less equaling that in large cities. This presents an ideal opportunity for the Wanda brand.

(3) To achieve marginal benefit

With the transition toward "light assets", our objective is to speed up development of the Wanda brand. We now open 26 new plazas (about five million square meters in total floor area) every year. It is an unprecedented – perhaps also unrepeatable – speed of development across the world. If history offers any guide, the real estate industry is inextricably linked to the urbanization process. Key urbanization developments in a country last for 20-30 years, and major real estate development opportunities will disappear once the urbanization process ends. Wanda is blessed with a golden opportunity amid China's urbanization, and we embraced the opportunity with thorough preparation. We will continue to step up our efforts and tap into the full potential of Chinese cities of varying sizes. From a financial perspective, asset-light businesses possess a favorable return on investment: the combined operating profit from two asset-light projects equals that of an asset-heavy project – assuming that the rental income of a standard asset-light project is 100 million yuan, Wanda will receive 70 million in rental revenue from every two asset-light projects (total profit 200 million yuan), which is roughly comparable to the average rental income (gross rental of 100 million yuan after deducting operating costs and taxes) of a standard asset-heavy project.

More importantly, rapid expansion of asset-light businesses will also lead to marginal benefits. Take Wanda Cinema Line, listed on the Shenzhen Stock Exchange, for example. Most Wanda cinemas operate within Wanda Plazas and have enjoyed fast development driven by the rapid growth of Wanda Commercial Properties as a whole. As another example, we are currently working on KIDSPLACE, the first comprehensive child entertainment project in China, integrating amusement park, education, food and retail businesses. We developed it because the absence of amenities for children would result in an age gap among Wanda Plaza customers. Our data show that the addition of children's facilities results in double-digit growth in customer traffic.

Why do we decide to do it ourselves? It is because that there is no partner able to keep pace with us. Children's business operators in China focus either on games or retail, and none of them integrate different businesses. We also talked with foreign companies in Europe, Japan and South Korea, but they were afraid of entering the Chinese market. Even if they come here, they can't do it that fast. Opening a couple of stores every year is far too slow for us, so we decided to do it ourselves. Founded last year, Wanda Children Entertainment opened nine stores in just one year. Given the rate of development of Wanda Plaza, KIDSPLACE will soon grow into the world's largest children's entertainment business. Furthermore, the expanding Wanda Plaza network will also benefit our O2O and Internet finance operations in terms of generating more resources.

3. How to make asset-light operations effective?

(1) A standard asset-light module

With the asset-heavy model, Wanda Commercial Properties focused on profit as the main criteria in local branch assessment, with the house price serving as the main indicator of the suitability of local markets for investment. In the case of the asset-light model, investment target selection is appraised mainly on investment cost and rental income instead. Wanda has developed hundreds of real estate projects over the past 20 years throughout the country, and has a clear understanding of the construction costs in different regions. First, we attach great importance to cost analysis, and spend one full year in developing four versions (A, B, C and D) of cost standards for each project. Furthermore, cost standards for southern cities with good geological conditions are different from those implemented at "soft foundation" areas. Similarly, two distinctive cost standards have been developed for northern cities according to geological differences.

In the past, the development of new Wanda Plazas was led by the development department, which was responsible for local project negotiations and project data collection. New projects were reviewed by the cost control department based on cost and profit analyses. The two departments then debated over the feasibility of the projects, and only with the consent from both sides, the proposal was submitted to the president and chairman for approval. After the introduction of the asset-light model, the decision now rests with the business management company with rental revenue as the sole criteria. As the manager of Wanda Plaza, the business management company makes conservative projections of leasing revenue. As a further precaution, we asked the commercial property research department to work out a set of rental estimation models for local markets, based on which separate projections are conducted independently. If the results of the two departments match each other, the project in question is considered highly reliable. And if there are significant discrepancies between the findings, the project will be sent back for reconsideration. As such, a complete set of standard modules is in place for asset-light investment operations.

(2) Project management reforms

Our project management model has also gone through several major reforms in a bid to expedite asset-light development. In the past, the project management process used to be complicated and time consuming, involving bidding, budgeting and final accounting. It proved too inefficient to keep pace with project development after the rollout of the asset-light strategy. For this reason, we introduced the turnkey project model, which represents a major innovation in the management of Chinese real estate projects. It involves Wanda partnering with the four companies under China Construction Group in the joint development of four versions of Wanda Plaza project pricing schemes for different areas. Wanda pays standard prices to the builders, and they carry out construction in compliance with relevant standards and deliver turnkey projects according to schedule – Wanda only needs to assess project quality without being involved in subcontractor recruitment/management. The turnkey construction project model is very popular in developed countries, where a high degree of specialization and subdivision can be achieved, allowing the investor, builder and manager to focus on their own businesses. On the contrary, Chinese property developers emphasize "all round" capabilities and insist on taking on everything by themselves, ranging from investment, land purchase, design and construction. This is decided by the current development phase of the Chinese real estate market.

The benefits of turnkey projects include cost effectiveness – the project company used to recruit 60-70 people for each Wanda Plaza, and the turnkey model has led to a two-thirds cut in headcount. There is also improved efficiency and a facilitated management process. This leads to win-win development – in turnkey projects, the builders become general contractors, whereas they used to be responsible only for civil works (accounting for no more than 50% of the total project cost), with Wanda taking charge of subcontracting for façade, interior decoration, mechanical and electrical operations. The new model lets the builders reap all construction revenues (including a certain amount of management fees charged on subcontractors) and higher profits. Therefore, turnkey projects are warmly welcomed by our strategic partners. It also enables Wanda to eliminate project corruption altogether. Needless to say, all subcontractors must be selected from our brand database.

(3) IT-based business management

The dramatic development speed of Wanda makes many people worried about a possible "hard landing" in the future. After the introduction of the asset-light strategy, the workload of business management increased against a reduction in project management operations. We currently launch over 20 Wanda Plazas a year, and this will be doubled from next year onward. How can Wanda manage to keep pace with the increased development speed? Business management has therefore become the decisive factor to our lasting success.

Given the large number of Wanda Plazas in China, it is simply impossible to manage all of them manually. We have built a fully developed IT-based management system. Our highly innovative "HuiYun" intelligent business information management system was officially rolled out in all Wanda Plazas across China in 2014, after a trial run in 2013. Integrating 16 sub-systems (covering fire management, mechanical and electrical management, energy management and operations management) into one intelligent platform, HuiYun, enables us to control all aspects of business management via a single computer monitor.

A high concentration of catering services is one of the most salient features of Wanda Plazas, and 30-40 restaurants can be found in every plaza. Ten years ago, I said the success of Wanda Plaza was not because we sold well, but because we served the diners well. Catering facilities necessarily result in increased fire hazards. To address the risks, we developed a kitchen automatic fire extinguishing system jointly with the national fire department. The system has been granted a global patent. It measures the temperature in the kitchen and cuts off the gas supply automatically, if the warning threshold is triggered; if the temperature continues to rise, automatic sprinklers will be activated to prevent fire accidents.

As well as supporting business management operations and ensuring security, the IT-based system also serves to reduce management costs. In the past, managing a 150,000 square-meter plaza required 131 employees, but now it has come down to 80 (a 40% headcount cut).

(4) Asset-light financing channels

How are Wanda's asset-light businesses funded? (One way is through external financing channels, e.g. funds, insurance companies and other institutional investors) thus far, we have concluded 25 legally binding projects, meaning over 100 projects can be executed as and when needed. There are also internal financing channels – the company has set up its own ecommerce company and acquired 99bill.com. Both companies are in the midst of developing brand new wealth management products, and product release is planned for next month. This will provide financing through crowdfunding for asset-light operations at Wanda Plazas. The investment targets of Wanda's financial products are real entities, thereby ensuring a reliable return for investors. We project that the cash return will be 6% on an annualized basis. Each Wanda Plaza will be disposed of in five to seven years, and the resulting earnings will be shared among the investors. Disposal is conducted through two methods, capitalization or sale. Real estate investment trusts (REITS) are now being tried in China, with pilot programs in progress in many cities. Wanda's financial products are designed as quasi-REITS, and even if REITS turn out to be unviable five years later when the Wanda Plaza becomes fully developed and generates high rental income, it can still be sold at a favorable price. Factoring in both the sale proceeds and yearly cash return, the annualized ROI of Wanda Plaza is estimated to be over 10%. If an investor has a financial emergency and needs to withdraw his investment urgently, he may sell the products on the warrant trading platform (we have agreed with two financial reform pilot zones to set up such a platform, and the market maker has also been appointed) – our financial products are liquid and can be traded one month after purchase. The investors also agree with Wanda Ecommerce and 99bill that a certain amount of earnings will be paid upon disposal of Wanda Plaza. This way, profits will be guaranteed for the e-commerce company. If successful, our financial products will offer funding for asset-light projects, thereby minimizing reliance on external investors.

The asset-light transition of Wanda Commercial Properties is not a random, arbitrary decision as it may seem. Instead, it is our conclusion after a lengthy process of studies and analyses on the cost standard module, turnkey model, IT system and financing channels. We have made thorough preparations for over a year, but the decision was only recently announced.

4. Objectives of the asset-light strategy

We have set out two strategic targets for asset-light projects. The first is increasing the number of Wanda Plazas to 400-500 by 2020, a nearly two-fold increase from the original target (240-250) under the asset-heavy model. By 2025, we strive to open 1,000 plazas in China. It may sound unrealistic that we will be able to launch 100 new plazas every year in five years. But this is indeed a completely realistic goal given our current execution capability, especially considering the growth in this ability over the next five years. For those who are suspicious, let us wait and see. Our second target is that by 2020, two-thirds of net profit at Wanda Commercial Properties will come from leasing businesses. It would be inappropriate to call a company a real estate developer if more than two-thirds of its net profit is contributed by businesses other than property sales. Therefore, we plan to remove "Properties" from the company's name, and rename it "Wanda Commercial Investment" or "Commercial Investment Management". This will mark the completion of the shift away from the real estate-reliant model, and reintroduce Wanda Commercial Properties as a service operator.

Thank you!

Chapter Eleven

Transformation

Four Transformation Phases

21 April, 2015 – A speech at the China Green Companies Summit

On 21 April 2015, Mr. Wang Jianlin spoke at the China Green Companies Summit. His speech focused on Wanda Group's fourth transformation. The following is a record of his speech:

The word "transformation" is popular right now, but the truth is, the issue of structural adjustment of industries has already been brought up over a decade ago at the 13th plenary session of the 6th Central Committee. It has also been a perpetual theme in the development of enterprises. It is impossible for any kind of enterprise and any form of business model to remain the same and not be eliminated eventually. Of the top 500 companies 30 years ago, less than 20% remain among today's top 500 companies. Perhaps in another 20 years, only a few of that 20% will remain. Hence, enterprises have to adapt to change, proactively change, and be adept at changing. Our main topic today is the transformation of Wanda Group.

I. The four transformations of Wanda

The first transformation occurred in 1993, when Wanda turned from a locally oriented enterprise into a country-wide enterprise. We stepped out from Dalian and expanded to Guangzhou, which was China's favored place for reforms. There was a popular saying at that time, "north, south, east, west and central (zhong). To find riches, go to Guangdong." It was a big step for us and took much courage. But with the experiences that came with that step, Wanda expanded nationwide on a large scale in 1998.

The second transformation was in the year 2000, when focus shifted from residential properties to commercial properties. There was instability in residential properties, with cash flow present only where projects existed; once projects were completed, cash flow stopped. Furthermore, judging by global trends, in every country, the city formation process takes about half a century. Once the urbanization process is completed, the property development industry shrinks. After taking into consideration prospects for continued stable growth, Wanda decided to shift its focus to commercial property.

A third transformation took place in 2006. Instead of specializing on just the property business, Wanda took on a composite business scope covering commercial property and cultural tourism, and which revolved around immovable assets. This transformation made us change our paradigms, talent structure and management. In the past, the management of Wanda was mostly made up of people from the field of construction. After changing our business scope, Wanda attracted talents from the tourism industry and cultural fields.

The fourth transformation was implemented in 2014. This time, it consisted of two parts: In terms of space, Wanda turned from a domestic enterprise into a multinational one; in terms of business content, Wanda changed from a real estate based enterprise into a service-based one, with operations in four main industries: Commercial property, culture, finance, and departmental stores. Wanda's fourth transformation was an intense one and involved profound changes. It differs fundamentally from the three previous transformations. Firstly, the nature of the enterprise underwent fundamental changes. Wanda remained focused on real estate throughout previous transformations, but this time, the focus shifted to services instead. Secondly, the strategic targets are different. Rather than just aiming to become a leader in China, Wanda looks to become a world-class multinational company.

II. Rationale behind the fourth transformation

1. Gaining greater competitiveness

In the past, some have likened Wanda's involvement in commercial property to the construction of a city moat. In this sense, Wanda's fourth transformation would be akin to "widening and deepening the moat" to increase competitiveness. Wanda has now taken the top spot in China in terms of immovable assets. The company opened 26 malls this year, increasing the property area held by five million square meters, while other players in the industry typically open no more than two malls in a year. In 2015, Wanda's total property area held reached 25 million square meters, and Wanda became the enterprise with the largest total leasable property space in the world. Since Wanda implemented the asset-light business model, the growth rate of its malls increased by multiples. By 2020, the total business real estate held or managed by Wanda will be comparable to the total held by the world's top holders of immovable assets. Wanda is set to at least eliminate competition within China.

Why did Wanda use the asset-light strategy? Wanda's heavy assets weren't doing badly – Wanda invests in itself, collects all rent and enjoys property capital appreciation. However, heavy assets are debt-heavy and cannot be developed quickly enough. Wanda has developed 109 malls, a large number for an enterprise, but far from adequate considering China's market of 1.4 billion people. To gain a greater edge, we have to penetrate third- and fourth-tier cities where others dare not venture, spreading through cities of all sizes in China and taking control of all physical commercial space. Wanda's strategy of expanding into other industries like culture, tourism, sports, etc. does not just serve to increase its competitiveness, but aims to eliminate competition as well.

2. Freedom from the effects of economic cycles

Economic ups and downs are inevitable in economies throughout the world and nobody can stop them. China is currently facing a downward cycle that began in 2013, and there has been no significant improvement. This shows that the current cycle is not over and the downturn is still dominant . Economic cycles deliver fatal blows to cyclical industries, and real estate is a typical cyclical industry. When a negative cycle hits the economy, property becomes very difficult to sell, no matter how much sellers lower prices; the property buyer mentality is to buy in a rising market. China's real estate market went through two downturns in 1993–1995 and 2007–2008. During those times, survival became extremely difficult for enterprises. Wanda underwent transformation to make itself immune to economic cycles. In its asset-light business model, Wanda's mall developments use investment funds from institutional investors or funds raised through investment products. With no property purchases involved, and with Wanda's mall business being cycle-resistant because it targets mass consumers, the performance of Wanda's mall investments has little to do with the rise and fall of property prices. This is how Wanda avoids being affected by economic cycles.

Why did Wanda go into the cultural industry and sports industry? The cultural industry in the U.S. accounts for 24% of GDP. U.S. top exports are not weapons and passenger planes, but cultural products, which include movies, music, comics and book copyrights etc. Currently, the cultural industry in China accounts for just 3% of GDP. In 2014, the size of the American sports industry was close to US$500 billion. In contrast, China's sports industry has yet to be developed. Its related industries, like sportswear and shoes, total only about 300 billion yuan, a tenth of that of the Americans. The average per-capita spend on sports in the U.S. is fifty times higher than in China. The cultural and sports industries in China are just starting to take off, and there is huge space for future development. In addition, these industries are not prone to the effects of economic cycles. Sometimes, the consumption of sports and cultural products actually increases during economic downturns – people go to the movies or watch sports on TV to relieve stress related to a negative economy.

Wanda is aggressively pushing into third- and fourth-tier cities using its asset-light strategy because of the higher consumer loyalty in these cities. Wanda has opened seven malls in Shanghai, and we are planning for a total of 20. However, our business influence can only reach a fraction of Shanghai's population, and some areas are already saturated. The situation is different in third- and fourth-tier cities. One Wanda mall is enough to cover the entire population of one city. Take for example, Langfang, in Hebei province. Its urban population is just under 400,000, but there are 40,000 to 50,000 customers at the local Wanda Plaza every day, about one-seventh of the city's population. And in Wanzhou, Chongqing, the local government at one time repeatedly invited Wanda to build a mall in the city. However, research conducted by Wanda's development department was negative. Wanzhou has a population of only 400,000, and the region was classified as economically backward. Nevertheless, I took into consideration the local government's enthusiasm and decided to go ahead with the investment anyway. At that time, I decided that if the investment was not successful, we could write it off as a form of contribution to the alleviation of poverty. Surprisingly, when Wanzhou's Wanda Plaza began operations, it broke Wanda's record for volume of mall patrons upon opening. Over 1.1 million people visited the mall in its first three days, which means most Wanzhou residents visited the mall a few times over three days. Many third- and fourth-tier cities lack comprehensive consumer hubs and good hotels, and these are what Wanda builds as soon as it enters these areas, and which become the first choice of consumers. The rate of return from rental investments is also higher in third- and fourth-tier cities compared with that of first- and second-tier cities.

3. Relationship between four main industries in which Wanda is involved

Wanda currently has operations in commercial property, cultural tourism, finance and departmental stores. Whether Wanda employs asset-light or asset-heavy methods of development, these four industries support and complement one another. Previously, Wanda developed cinemas, electronic game arcades and discount KTVs (karaoke systems) in order to provide mall customers with a vibrant experience, and this required substantial support from cultural and entertainment fields. In recent years, Wanda has been searching for a development partner that can incorporate children's entertainment into its malls, allowing them to be able to cater to patrons of all ages. There is currently no company in the country that provides comprehensive services for children – most only specialize in one particular area like children's retail, entertainment, or education. Foreign companies who have what Wanda needs are unwilling to operate in China, and even if they are, they develop at the rate of one outlet per year or one every two years, which is insufficient. We have no choice but to develop our own one-stop comprehensive service for children, and we named it "Kid's Place". It combines children's entertainment, retail, education, as well as food and beverages. Kid's Place was set up last year with nine outlets, and 2015 will see over 30 opening up. With assorted services for children, there has been a significant increase in customer volume at Wanda's malls. From now on, Kid's Place will be a standard item in Wanda's malls. Since Wanda's commercial property business adopted the asset-light strategy, our malls have seen rapid expansion. Hence the number of children's entertainment outlets is set to increase, and the growth of cinemas will accelerate as well.

Under the asset-heavy business model, Wanda opens over 20 malls in a year. After Wanda's transformation into the asset-light model, 50 malls can be opened next year. Our highest target is 100 malls in a year. By 2020, two-thirds of Wanda's revenue from commercial property will come from rental. Wanda will then no longer be a real estate development company, and market valuation will change. By the time Wanda's malls are spread throughout all provincial capitals, prefectural-level cities and counties, it will have a yearly consumer volume of over 10 billion, covering a population base of 700 to 800 million; all consumer data for China's primary consumers will be in the possession of Wanda. Consumer data held by Wanda not only consists of shopper data, but also includes data from other realms such as cultural, entertainment and food and beverage. Compared with the typical e-retailer, our consumer data is more complete and accurate. This provides the best foundation for Wanda's Internet finance business. At the same time, we are developing a point of sale (POS) system that allows us to monitor the hundreds of POS terminals in each mall. We will be able to obtain data on each retailer's cash flow, and Wanda's Internet financing can provide loans for them based on a daily repayment system. Compared with traditional banks, such an operation has lower costs and lower risks. Hence, Wanda's transformation allows the four industries it is involved in to support one another and mutually add value.

III. Reasons behind the fourth transformation

1. Change of trends in the industry

A turning point has been seen in China's property market – a state of balance between supply and demand will emerge. This turning point is not V-shaped but is shaped more like an elongated "L". China's property market will never be able to offer the buyer instant profits again – the era where you can get rich while lying on your back is gone. This is our long-term view of the trend of the property market, and Wanda cannot continue on the asset-heavy path that relies on sales for cash-flow and investments in Wanda malls, because the property market will gradually return to offering only average returns.

2. To be consistent with China's national strategy

The entire Chinese economy is going through transformations and structural adjustment, and the country is willing to pay the price. The main objective of transformation is to achieve a state of economic growth that is based on domestic demand. Currently, 60% of products made in China are exported, and only 40% are consumed domestically. This means that for every 100 yuan worth of goods produced, 60 has to come from foreign demand to support China's economic growth. In contrast, 85% of American products are consumed domestically, and in most developed economies, domestic consumption rates are in excess of 80%. If China can achieve the same consumption rate as developed countries, its macro-economy will be much more stable. China will also become the world's largest consumer, which will give China a greater say in international affairs. Wanda's transformation is consistent with China's economic strategy. Investment does not mean increasing production capacity, the four main industries in which Wanda is involved are modern service industries encouraged by the government. Increasing investments in them while expanding their scope and increasing domestic demand is exactly what China's economic transformation requires.

3. Wanda's enterprise culture

Wanda is an enterprise that keeps on evolving, one that is constantly reinventing itself. It is an inherent enterprise culture that continuously recreates itself. Only in this way can new business models be discovered, long-term cash flow achieved, profits increased, and safety of the enterprise ensured. We are working to achieve what we set as a company slogan 20 years ago, "Wanda International, an enterprise spanning a century." In practice, Wanda has been tirelessly innovating towards a business ecosystem where its operations in four main industries can support one another and grow together. Wanda will continue to be outstanding for a long time to come, whether I am here or not. Dell once said that his greatest contribution in life is having established a great organization. My own dream is to make my greatest contribution not only establishing a great organization, but also making it so that the organization will continue to grow healthily when I'm not around anymore.

Wanda's transformations were not haphazard moves, nor were they steps taken out of impetus, but carefully planned and proactive transformations with clear goals. For instance, Wanda's 2006 decision to go into the cinema business. At that time, box-office takings for the entire country was less that one billion yuan, and industry profits totaled less than 100 million. Such returns cannot support investments in the cinema business. However, our analysis showed that with the growth of consumer hubs, the cinema industry would see explosive growth, and we were proven right. The cinema market in China had 10 consecutive years of growth above 30%, with box-office takings totaling 29 billion yuan in 2014. Wanda's investment overseas provides another example. At a time when the negative effects of the 2008 financial crisis had yet to fully subside, we judged that it was a good opportunity for Wanda to make international acquisitions. In 2010, we started negotiations to acquire international cinemas and property as we felt that the global economy had hit rock bottom and it was a good time for acquisitions to be made at bargain prices. We bought AMC Entertainment in America at a very low price and made it profitable in the same year. We then listed it on the New York Stock Exchange in the second year, achieving a return of 400%. Wanda's acquisition of AMC shook the whole of Wall Street. Many had expected Wanda to fail badly in this venture, but it turned out to be the opposite.

Wanda had been looking for hotel investments in London. In 2011, there happened to be a bank auction for a hotel apartment. We negotiated with them and they agreed not to hold an auction if we could sign the acquisition agreement within a week. As we had been researching on investing in Europe and knew what we were doing, we agreed, on that same day, to acquire the project for over 90 million pounds. Now, the residential part of the project has been launched and response was very good. Not only do we now have a hotel worth hundreds of millions of pounds, we also have extra cash of tens of millions of pounds. Had it not been for our continuous research of the market, we would not have been able to spot such a good opportunity. As the old saying goes, "opportunity only looks for the ones who are prepared." Wanda has acquired premium projects in Madrid, Chicago, Los Angeles and Sydney. These did not come by chance. It was due to Wanda's transformation drive and preparedness that Wanda was able to seize opportunities.

IV. Goals of the fourth transformation

Wanda is an enterprise with great aspirations. Without aspirations, Wanda would not be where it is now. We still have aspirations.

1. To achieve stable, long-term cash flow

Wanda has set greater targets and implemented greater changes in the fourth round of transformation. The company hopes that mid-term goals will be reached in 2020: to have income from services and net profits taking up at least 65% of that of the entire organization, while income and net profit from sales of property make up no more than 35%; to have overseas revenue accounting for at least 20% of the total; we will attempt to reach 30%. If cash flow from commercial property, culture and tourism, finance and departmental stores can achieve high stability, Wanda will have an "iron square" that will guarantee the stability of the enterprise.

2. Upgrading of Wanda's asset structure

Firstly, Wanda has to become a modern service company. It has to shed all its involvement in real estate within five years and become a fully fledged high-tech service-based company.

Secondly, Wanda has to control upstream industry chains, as well as channels. Wanda sets clear targets when it steps into any industry. We do not take on low value-adding downstream roles in the industry, but control upstream chains and channels instead. For example, in the cinema industry, Wanda first built channels, followed by investing in movie-making and distribution. Once distribution and screening channels are secured, Wanda would have a say in the industry chain and not be subjected to restriction by others, thus maximizing profits. Wanda's entrance into the sports industry also involved controlling upstream chains, gaining core resources of copyrights and marketing rights. We acquired the world's second-largest sports marketing company, In-front Sports and Media AG, which held program copyrights and marketing rights of seven Winter Olympics events. All television and mobile device broadcasts of the events have to be approved by the company. In-front also has exclusive broadcast rights for the FIFA World Cup to Asia-Pacific regions. These are all core resources that are most valuable to a sports marketing company. Wanda plans to acquire two or three more sports marketing companies with unique core resources. Our goal is to become the largest sports marketing company in the world by the end of the year. More importantly, China's sports scene had only started taking off, and the country plans to grow the sports industry to reach a scale of five trillion yuan by 2025, which translates to a hundred-fold growth in ten years from today's 50 billion, a rather large cake to bake.

Similar to Wanda's investments in the cultural sector, Wanda's sports marketing company has plenty of room for growth.

3. To become a world-class multinational company

Wanda must achieve the "2211" goal by 2020, which means that the enterprise must have assets of at least US$200 billion, a market value of at least US$200 billion, revenue of US$100 billion and net profit of US$10 billion. Wanda must also achieve the status of a world-class multinational company, making a bright mark on the world map on behalf of China's enterprises, especially private ones.

Thank you, everyone!

Chapter Twelve

Going Global

Going Global, the Wanda Way

30 October, 2015 – An open lecture at Harvard University

I. Chairman Wang's speech

Harvard is a well-known university for its freedom of academics and thought. So there are no limits when it comes to the Q&A section, feel free to raise any question. Regarding Wanda Group, as Professor Shih said, we have a 27-year history from 1988, and in a month this year will be over. In 2015, I estimate that Wanda's asset will exceed US$100 billion and annual income will be around US$50 billion. Net profit and other core financial metrics will rank top among Chinese private companies.

We have three main businesses—commercial properties, cultural industry and corporate finance. Our development can be described in four stages. The first was in 1993, when we went outside Dalian and into the rest of the country, transforming from a regional company to a national company. This was a key step for us. At that time, people who didn't do business in China were not able to understand us. You couldn't get a license to work outside Dalian so you had to be affiliated to other companies to do business. However, I said that nothing is impossible if we keep an adventurous spirit.

From this critical step, our second stage was to transform Wanda from a pure housing company to a real estate company that holds properties. Over the past 20 years or so we've been changing and from the year 2000 our real estate subsidiary has become number one in the world. We have become huge in this industry, and we continue to grow. Nevertheless, we started another transformation in 2015. From now on we will no longer hold any properties and we will gradually transition into an "asset-light" model, but that is a whole other story.

Since 2006, we have undergone our third transformation. From a real estate company, we became a comprehensive company, entering the cultural and tourism industries. Over the past 10 years, Wanda's cultural industry has become the largest in China. To put that into context, the revenue from Wanda's cultural industry will exceed over 50 billion yuan. Of course, this is not comparable with the United States where there are many companies worth $10 billion. Not only are we number one in our region, but our worth exceeds that of the combined assets of the following nine companies in China. However, you should also know that there won't be a company worth US$100 billion in the cultural industry, or an annual income of US$50 billion or $100 billion. Though the cultural industry has a huge influence, the largest company in the world may reach over US$30 billion in revenue.

Now we are experiencing the fourth transformation since 2012. We are going global. We had this idea very early, around six or seven years ago. Before then we were not so ambitious – not until we purchased AMC in the US. In just three and a half short years we have invested over US$15 billion overseas. This year, our revenue from overseas business will reach 15% of our total revenue. We have also set a strategic target: by the year 2020, we will grow our total assets and be a public company worth over US$200 billion, our annual revenue will be US$100 billion within five years, and our net profits will reach over $10 billion. Of this $100 billion annual revenue, our revenue from overseas business will make up at least 30% of that total. This fourth transformation is the deepest transformation – from a Chinese company to not only an international company but also a top one. We will try hard to make Wanda a spokesperson for Chinese companies going abroad.

For example, we are trying to build our hotel brand right now. Of all luxury hotels in the world, none of them are Chinese, with the exception perhaps for Malaysian Robert Kuok who is ethnically Chinese. The biggest luxury item in the world is actually hotels, followed by yachts and airplanes. Bags and clothes, as luxury goods, are overstated. Can you say that expensive belts are luxury? They are high-end products, but they are not a luxury.

Wanda owns a lot of hotels. By the end of the year we will have around 100 five-star hotels, and around 100 additional hotels under construction. We decided to work with our own resources to establish our brands, because hotel brands will take more than 10 to 20 years to establish. So far we have hotels in seven landmark cities, such as London, Sydney and Madrid. We also have hotels in three major cities in the U.S.. All of them are located in the heart of the city. For example, our hotel in Chicago is in Millennium Park, just across the river. In New York we are on 5th Avenue, and our Los Angeles hotel is at the top of Beverly Hills.

We are building our luxury hotel brand, and this is just one side of our globalization strategy. Of course, we don't rely primarily on hotels. Generally speaking, although Wanda has been afforded a certain wealth and scale, we have not stopped to gain more wealth. We are not for personal consumption; my goal is to build Wanda into a hyperpower and use our resources to establish the largest individual charitable fund, to contribute not just to our country, but to all humankind.

This is my brief speech. Thank you very much.

II. Discussion with Professor Willy Shih

Shih: Well, Chairman Wang, I think that is incredibly ambitious, and I've been watching your company for some time. It's very interesting to me that you seem to be moving into two very different sectors from the traditional real estate development, sports and cultural industries, motion pictures. Let's talk about sports first. We see that you recently acquired the Infront Sports Media of Switzerland, Atletico Madrid and most recently the Ironman Triathlon. These are really very different holdings. Could you talk a little bit about your vision there?

Wang: Wanda Sports Company is already the largest sports company in the world in terms of income. There are few sports companies that make over US$10 billion. Generally speaking, a sports company with billions in annual income is seen as relatively large. Our dream is not about how large the company is but about improving China's sport industry by adapting to the development of China's economy and society. Of course, Wanda may realize an opportunity to expand its scale, increase profits and gain recognition from capital markets in the process. For example, China has over 1.3 billion people, but measured by American standards, revenue from China's sports industry may be less than US$30 billion. America's sports industry or the global sports industry is only about sports events, sports economy and sports communication, instead of the manufacture of sportswear and equipment. In contrast, America's sports industry attains a revenue of over US$500 billion, and it only has 300 million people. China's per capita is only 60%-70% of that of America's. As an emerging sector, China's sports industry has tremendous room to grow. At the beginning of this year, China's State Council formulated a plan that expects China's sports industry to reach a net worth of 500 billion yuan by 2025, which will come to around US$1 trillion or at least US$800 billion if the yuan appreciates. It means there is ample room to grow in China. So Wanda has not only bought the companies you mentioned before, we will conduct a series of acquisitions in sports. Our goal is to make sure that the businesses of acquired companies can touch down in the Chinese market and promote the development of this kind of sports industry.

Shih: Well, it's very ambitious. I was very interested to follow your acquisition of AMC theatres of US, you mentioned earlier that you're moving into cultural industries. That seems to be much harder than traditional Chinese manufacturing products, and I was wondering if you could do it – with this plus the sports industries we talked about, some of the challenge Wanda is facing is going global. You know, these are quite challenging industries to understand.

Wang: Of course, Chinese companies face a lot of challenges when they go global. Chinese companies have not gone abroad, that is to say, they have only just started to go abroad. Though there are around 100 Chinese companies on the Fortune Global 500 List, which is more or less similar to the US, the real transnational companies are rare. Basically, most of them are state-owned monopolies. China can only become truly prosperous once it deploys a number of top international companies and dominates international resources and markets. You mentioned the challenges that Chinese companies face when they go global, and also what we faced. Firstly, there will be a lot of contradictions when you deal with local laws, corporate culture and management. Actually, the most difficult part was our first step to acquire AMC in 2012. At that time, I believed that our company scale was relatively large and had strong informatization capabilities, and we also had some experiences in management. Besides, we had negotiated this project for over two years, and had prepared enough managerial personnel and technology. We succeeded in this first step. Regarding Wanda's globalization, or rather the globalization of Chinese companies, it's an inevitability. If Chinese companies don't go through the globalization phase, it's hard for us to make China powerful or realize the Chinese Dream.

Shih: Yeah, it's quite challenging. I see you've really taken on some difficult cross boundaries and many different fields. You know, the track record frankly for many companies going abroad is very mixed if you will. Maybe you can comment on that because it's a very hard problem.

Wang: I believe the biggest problem in the globalization is dealing with the original management, how to retain them and let them work hard. There must be original management when you acquire a company. I don't think it's a financial matter or a case of informatization management from afar. In my view, these are all easy to resolve. Is how to mobilize the initiative of original management the biggest problem? If you buy a company but all the original management leave, you've probably already failed. All the companies that Wanda have acquired have one thing in common, which is that Wanda didn't assign anyone to the company, including AMC. By designing a reasonable and effective incentive system, you can make management work hard for you. Take AMC as an example: we designed a good incentive system, which allowed them to make a loss in the first two years and make gains in the last three years. As a result, AMC made a profit in their first year once we came on board. And management's income has increased 20%-30% for three consecutive years, which is hard to do in the US. So the most important thing in globalization is to keep the original team. When an American company acquires a Chinese company, they usually send in a team of Americans, and this is destined to fail. In short, I think the biggest problem is how to mobilize the original management's initiative and work for the new shareholder.

Shih: OK. Let me try another one. We've recently seen a lot of capital outflow out of China. I've heard some people kind of skeptical behind Wanda's increasing overseas investments, as we heard of you making a lot of purchases. So the skeptic thinks you increase overseas investment because you want to diversify assets overseas. Maybe you could comment on that, overseas versus Chinese economy. Is it just getting money out of the country?

Wang: Firstly, the actual reason for overseas investment is asset transfer, or rather to add assets overseas. That's the result. However, there are no right or wrong answers on asset transfer from overseas investment, just legal or illegal. For example, you had a meal today. How can you say that it's right or wrong to have a meal? It's wrong only if you use public money to have a meal. If you use your own money, that's alright. It's the same logic.

Secondly, private companies that go global to expand their business are answering the call from government. At the end of last year, China's State Council specifically released specifications to guide private companies going global. It can be said that Wanda answered that call.

Thirdly, Wanda didn't steal, rob, or print money. It is fully earned by ourselves. I can invest anywhere I want to. That investment freedom, or rather freedom of capital movement, is a basic measurement of a country's legal system. If a company doesn't have full investment autonomy, there is no freedom in that society.

Shih: So you made your money by selling to shoppers like me in Wanda Plaza or people staying in Wanda Hotels I guess. Let me ask just one more general question then I want to open questions to the floor. Do you have some views on the macro environment challenges facing the Chinese economy today?

Wang: The biggest pressure faced by China's macroeconomy is the pressure exerted on economic transformation. We used to have a saying in China, the "three engines of growth": investment, exports and consumption. Two of those engines are currently running on empty – investment has slowed and exports are declining. Although consumption has taken up some of the slack, we can see from last year's numbers that China's consumption accounted for 51% of GDP. This is particularly surprising. But as consumption grew by 1-2%, investment and exports shrank by 3-4% and the economy lost its pace. So from the outside looking in, perhaps from a European or American perspective, you might think that China's economy is crashing, but actually this couldn't be further from the truth. This is the necessary pain of economic transformation, and it is ten years long. I think it can be shortened to six or seven years, so I think we can get it to five years at most before we can emerge from the pain. When consumption accounts for two thirds of China's GDP, I think our problems will be resolved.

Q & A

Q: Thank you very much for your comments. At international level, corporate level, and also Chinese companies' globalization, that is very significant for all the Chinese companies coming abroad. So far, we know that Chinese national level gives policies in Asia and also Europe. So for capital outflow, for example, we have AIIB (Asian Infrastructure Investment Bank) in Asia. We have "One Belt One Road" in Europe. But the Chinese government didn't explicitly offer a policy on capital outflow in US. Wanda is actually a pioneer company doing this. So I wonder, what is the implication for Wanda's movement to Chinese government policy? Do you think in the future the Chinese government will use your movement as a reference for the policy in China and other Chinese companies coming abroad? Thank you.

A: Well, I'm flattered. If Wanda could be so important to Chinese government and be used by the government in some way, I would feel very happy. The first time when I came to purchase AMC Entertainment, there were newspapers saying that I was acting on behalf of China and the money came from my country. This rumor disappeared because I've purchased more assets here, maybe. In fact, it is understandable as people may not understand when Chinese companies go global. In the future, if China has one or two hundred outstanding cross border globalized Chinese companies in the world, then there will no longer be this kind of opinion or skepticism. State-owned corporations may represent the will of the state, though in fact a lot of them are market-driven in China. As a privately owned corporation, we basically have to use our own judgement; the first objective is to make money. As said previously, we don't have a banknote printing factory and we have to make profit through prudent management. When you want to buy something, you know good stuff comes with a good price. If you want better, you pay more. Overall, when you've purchased a good company with a high price, you need to make good profit out of it through excellent management. It's all on us. So my answer to your question is to be suspicious about all things that don't seem right. And I am the founder and largest shareholder of Dalian Wanda Group, also the final decision maker.

Q: Thank you for coming. I'm so excited about the purchase of AMC Theater on your behalf and would love to know what your future plans are? And how does China plan for it as it increasingly has more global share of the move economy? How do you think the future of the movie industry will look? And how can you shape it?

A: It's difficult to answer a question at this level. I am the chairman of Dalian Wanda Group and AMC is just another subsidiary under Wanda Cultural Industry Group, which in Chinese is my "grandchild level". So the decision of how it's going to be developed should come from the senior management and that is CEO of Wanda Cultural Industry Group. I need to manage and formulate corporate strategies, the strategic direction, or being the final approval level on major investments; for example, how much capital investment. It's difficult for me to go into details. I trust that our professional managers working in Wanda manage very well.

Q: My question is very simple. Building a company like Wanda has always been my dream. As a successful person are you clear what you are doing? Like what's your next step, what's your goal?

A: Do you think I'm really successful? I believe I'm still on my way to get where I want to be. I mean it. The way I defined success for myself is to let Wanda to become a world renowned company or be in the top 10. That's my dream. Now, Wanda might have gained some awareness globally, but it's still far from being a real international brand. I hope that, in the future, when people are talking about Wanda, it could be like they are talking about Microsoft, Apple, or Walmart nowadays. Everyone knows what it is. To build a top brand as a leading Chinese enterprise is my dream. Speaking of when I could achieve it, maybe in four or five years the fastest, or seven to eight years at a slower pace. I will retire by then. My other dream is to help a poverty relief mission in China and to really make a difference for it. I've taken care of a prefecture in Guizhou Province as an experiment and promised 3,000,000 residents there that the Per Capita Income would double in five years in that prefecture. We don't simply give away money, but have done two years' research. We've tried to build it through two main methods:

first, to establish a vocational college as residents who have a diploma from a vocational college will be able to find jobs; second, to help develop its distinctive industry – tea. We will expand the tea planting and processing system, along with branding strategies, to make fortune for everyone there.

Q: Hi, my name is Nick and thank you so much for coming all the way to Harvard. I don't know if you've been following presidential election; for next year, I mean as far as I can see, Hillary Clinton is fighting really hard against Donald Trump, but she's probably going to win next year. My question would be, what do you think, under her administration, the trading policy in the States is going to change, regarding US-China relations and what do you think the influence would be, either in China, or in your corporation? Thank you.

A: Unlike Americans, the Chinese focus on our own affairs. America has a problem of involving matters of other countries. I heard that two of thirds of the Congressional agenda are about problems and issues outside of the States. So the election is of no relevance to me? I believe that no matter who wins the election, the President of the USA won't do anything to harm the China-US relationship as the economy connection between our two countries is just getting stronger and stronger. For example, a company like Wanda, we've hired 20,000 staff in the States as we are developing here. Imagine that one day, if there are 100 Chinese companies offering 20 million jobs in the States, why couldn't China and the US embrace in a great relationship? So it's been said, it doesn't matter who wins the presidency, as long as it's good for both our countries.

Q: Hi, Mr. Wang, I am a freshman at Harvard Business School. I'm wondering what is Wanda's core competitiveness for its development abroad. How do you address the problem that you are not very familiar with overseas markets? Thank you.

A: Speaking of Wanda's core competitiveness in the overseas market, I think the first advantage could be we have money. Why? Because as the economy develops, the cash flow runs stronger and stronger, so we need to purchase more assets. The second is, in Wanda, I am the largest shareholder and also the final decision maker and I'd like to drive the company with long-term strategy and help our company achieve its value through efficient management. This is different from funds in the capital market that people purchase for selling. The third is my management skills gained through a few decades in developing the corporation, knowing how to check cost and profit daily and weekly by informatization and remote-communication system, not just getting the final figures at the end of a year.

Q: Hello. You have very ambitious plans and I'm sure you will be active for many more years. But when you retire, how would you want to be remembered? If there is just one thing that people would remember you for, what would you want it to be?

A: Well, the thing I most want is this: Wang Jianlin won't be hated by anyone, or not be remembered. There might be cultural a difference between US and China, that in China, it's difficult to make people really like you and remember you for a long time. Right now, China is still in the transformation phase where some people could act flightily. They want to make a fortune, but sometimes may hate wealthy people. I do hope that people can picture a philanthropist in their mind, not an entrepreneur when I retire or grow old. I would be thankful of being able to contribute to philanthropy.

Q: As you expand the Wanda hotel portfolio both domestically in China and abroad, how do you see the customer base changing? Do you think the client you are seeking to add is going to become more international? Or do you think it's going to be a Chinese client that's travelling more abroad and frequently in your hotels around the world?

A: For domestic hotels in China, Chinese customers certainly are our targets, while international customers are our focus for hotels aboard. The objective of establishing Wanda hotels is not to offer places for Chinese tourists going abroad, but to build up a real high-end Chinese hotel brand. This is also the reason that why Wanda hasn't gone for acquisition of Starwood in the recent case that has been mentioned for about $12bn. It's still Starwood even if we purchase it. I'd rather spend more time in building our own brand, step by step. $2bn could be enough for it, not $12bn.

Q: Hello Mr. Wang. You mentioned that our country is in a period of economic transformation. Can you give us students a general suggestion, as we have varying amounts of time left before graduation: what kinds of opportunities will be there for us during this transition when we come home?

A: The greatest opportunities in China lie in its service industry – not the traditional service industry, but a modern service industry. Personally, I think there are three particularly promising industries. The first is in entertainment. You can see China's economy is now growing at 6-7%, but for the past six years the entertainment industry has been growing by over 40%, and this year it has topped 50%. There are certainly broad prospects for the future of the entertainment industry in China. The second industry is sports. I mentioned previously that the sports industry in China is currently realising an annual income of US$20-30 billion, and that's not even factoring in its potential if we grow to the same scale as the US. There is room to grow several dozen times over. This is especially so if we look to contemporary China, where we pursue health and longevity. So the sports industry in China has a bright future, absolutely. If you can study marketing, economics or media in the field of sports, this will be very useful as current talent in those areas is scarce. The third industry is tourism, particularly in the integration of online to offline models, or O2O. This integrated tourism industry innovates by combining the travel destination with offline and online channels. Within the next 10 years, these three industries will experience a significant growth in income. Enter those industries no matter what you major in – there is much money to be made there.

Q: Could you please comment on the implication of the recent revocation of the One Child Policy on the real estate market?

A: It's good, but a bit late.

Q: I wanted to ask a question just now about whether Wanda's hotels were biased towards foreigners or Chinese people. But I want to ask, in the US, or perhaps throughout the Western world, there is a perception that Chinese products and services are considered to be inferior. This is very sad for Chinese people, very shameful. As your company heads abroad, how do you face such a problem? What strategy do you have to change certain foreign stereotypes around our products and services?

A: You began to ask about hotels, and then you went onto some bigger questions. First, for hotels, the high-end talent in this industry is mostly foreigners, both in China and abroad. No matter where you come from, it's ok that you get paid well to work for me. Secondly, regarding China's service transformation, Wanda cannot do it alone. Many Chinese companies need to work together to achieve this. This is the first step. Have America's products always been so good? I heard a story today that in the 1970s and 1980s Japanese cars entered the US market and Americans couldn't sell their cars fast enough to get their hands on a Japanese model. Nowadays you have American entrepreneurs who come out and wonder why they aren't patriotic, and so on. American cars back then must have been big, bulky gas-guzzlers, and Japanese cars were better. So under the impact of Japanese cars, American cars changed gears and clawed themselves back into the market. Thirty years ago this would have been a pipedream. Quality and services in China are little lacking right now, but they are in the inevitable stages of development. Don't worry, I believe that we can solve this problem.

Q: Hello Mr. Wang, I'm from Boston University. My question today is: you mentioned earlier in your talk that Wanda encountered some local cultural and legal difficulties when you were going global. Previously, Wanda's plan to rebuild the Espana Building was rejected by the Spanish government; do you have any response to this? And how do you regard local legal or cultural problems as Wanda goes international? Thank you.

A: First, let me make a correction: it was not the Spanish government that vetoed the proposal, it was a personal campaign against us by Madrid. This is a perfect example of freedom in the West: anyone can express their view and use signatures on a website to protest our rebuilding efforts. It was not the government that rejected the plan. Secondly, you are bound to encounter problems, whether it be through investment or through the development process. It is a very normal occurrence. If there is no problem, then there is no need for a boss or a highly paid professional manager. What do you do when you encounter a problem? You be patient. Slowly, they state their reasons. You can give me suggestions, and I can hire a PR team or lawyers to rebut you, right? This matter is still ongoing, and we wait patiently for an outcome.

Wang Jianlin was born on October 24, 1954, soon after China's Communist revolution. He was raised in Cangxi County as the eldest of five brothers.

His father was a war veteran of the Red Army and at 15 years old Wang followed in his father's footsteps by enrolling in the People's Liberation Army in 1970. He left the army in 1986 and formed a property company in the north-eastern city of Dalian.

Today, Wang Jianlin serves as the Chairman of the Dalian Wanda Group, the world's biggest property developer, as well as the world's largest movie theatre operator.